PRAISE FOR *PR*

"Mary Nelson speaks from her ov   ce in praying with many others, when   God can bring you healing from canc   ion, and the busyness of dealing wi   it to pray, or when cancer challenges your faith, this book will help you put words to your prayers as you seek to connect with God. May this book strengthen your trust in God as He walks with you through—and beyond—your experience of cancer."

—Carol Peters-Tanksley, M.D., D.Min., OB-Gyn Physician,
Ordained Christian Minister,
Author of *Dr. Carol's Guide to Women's Health*

"When your 'mission is remission' like mine, prayer is the prescription. Read *Praying for the Cure* through every treatment, every challenge, every tear, and every triumph, and be reminded that God's love is sufficient to cover any diagnosis."

—Pat Williams, Senior Vice President of the Orlando Magic, Author,
Speaker, Cancer Survivor

"I never asked for the label of Common Trauma Expert; however, God knew from the beginning that He would provide a powerful purpose through my pain. This is why I appreciate *Praying for the Cure*. . . . If you want to know what God *really* thinks about this dreaded illness and those struck by its insidious tentacles, you must read *Praying for the Cure*—the truth may surprise you."

—Anita Agers Brooks, Inspirational Business/Life Coach,
International Speaker, Award-Winning Author of *Getting Through
What You Can't Get Over* and Other Published Titles

"*Praying for the Cure* will restore your trust and faith in Jehovah-Rapha, the God who heals. Be encouraged and uplifted as you enter into the loving presence of the Ultimate Comforter. Then may you say. . .'It is well with my soul.' "

—Sue Johnson, Pray for the Cure Prayer Minister, Hosanna!
Lutheran Church and 16-Year Breast Cancer Survivor

"As I experienced my own battle with cancer, I knew I wanted and needed to keep God close. I longed to hear His voice, and I wanted to talk to Him in return. But sometimes it was hard to know how to do that. Fear and doubt would enter my thoughts, creating 'static' on my lifeline to God. *Praying for the Cure* provides the perfect resource for clearing away the 'noise' that keeps us from connecting with the Father."

—Kris Bowe, Cancer Survivor,
Pray for the Cure Participant, and Prayer Minister

"Based on her own life story and her experience ministering to others, Mary has created a beautiful gift for those diagnosed with cancer. She not only guides us on a journey of hope but lifts us above our circumstances through the truths of Scripture and an intimate relationship with God."

—Julia Holtze, Adult Ministries Pastor, Hosanna!

"Mary Nelson once again has captured the art of bringing God's promises to life for anyone experiencing cancer or other serious health challenges of any kind. As a three-time cancer survivor (ovarian, kidney, and liver) and Care Pastor of a larger congregation, I cannot say enough about the hope, love, peace, clarity, empowerment and healing the book offers a cancer sufferer, a supportive friend or family member or anyone helping them medically or spiritually. When things in life are out of our control, God Himself can bring a powerful peace, filling us with trust instead of fear. The personalization of His Word and grace successfully turns an unknown future into a journey through every phase of life through His strength."

—Pat Moe, Care Ministries Pastor,
Hosanna! Church, Lakeville, MN

"Pastor Mary Nelson writes out of her personal experience, not untested theory or theology. She has boldly 'prayed for the cure' with thousands of brokenhearted and feeble-bodied people dealing with the daunting realities of cancer. Physical healing or not, her writing and ministry produce the greatest fruit of all: fortified faith and healed souls."

—Ryan Alexander, Lead Pastor of Hosanna! Church, Lakeville, MN

"Mary Nelson, in her new book *Praying for the Cure*, provides patients with a biblically-based guide to help them through their journey with cancer. The typical questions patients have such as, "Why did I get this disease?," "Is God punishing me?," and "Where is God in this illness?" are all beautifully addressed with prayer and scriptures. Patients start their journey with fear and questions but can finish it with hope and a new understanding of God's love for them after reading through the book. I would recommend *Praying for the Cure* for any believer dealing with cancer or any serious illness or circumstance. The book contains good advice for dealing with life."

—Theodore Sawchuk M.D., F.A.C.S, Urologic Surgeon,
Co-founder Burning Hearts Ministry, Fargo, ND

"Mary Nelson wrote her new book straight from Heavenly Father's Heart. Those who read, declare, and believe the truths in her book will go from misunderstanding and doubt about God's love and perfect plans to a place of belief, healing, and restoration. Mary's book is not only for those struggling with cancer but also for anyone going through a trial!"

—Mark and Kathy Strandjord, Cofounders of Spirit of Hope Minstries

PRAYING for the CURE

A Powerful Prayer Guide
for Comfort and Healing from Cancer

Mary J. Nelson

SHILOH RUN PRESS

An Imprint of Barbour Publishing, Inc.

Cover Design: Greg Jackson, Thinkpen Design

Published in association with the literary agency of Credo Communications, LLC, Grand Rapids, Michigan, www.credocommunications.net.

Published by Shiloh Run Press, an imprint of Barbour Publishing, Inc., P.O. Box 719, Uhrichsville, Ohio 44683, www.shilohrunpress.com

Our mission is to publish and distribute inspirational products offering exceptional value and biblical encouragement to the masses.

Member of the
Evangelical Christian
Publishers Association

Printed in the United States of America.

Dedication

All the glory to *Jehovah-Rapha*, the God who heals, who rescued me from the pit of cancer, set my feet on solid ground, and gave me a new song to sing. May I tell the world of Your glorious deeds and sing Your praises forever.

Acknowledgments

For inspiring me to write this book, I honor the thousands of courageous men, women, and their families and friends who have attended Pray for the Cure at Hosanna! Church in Lakeville, Minnesota, to seek the Lord for a cure in the battle against cancer. It has been our great privilege to pray with you, encourage you, and walk with you through this unexpected journey toward healing, wholeness, and freedom. A special thank you to the Pray for the Cure prayer team for your faithful obedience to this ministry.

If you are interested in starting
a Pray for the Cure ministry in your church,
contact Mary J. Nelson at mary@prayforthecure.net

Contents

Barbara

Breathe God deep into your
lungs
Listen to His whispers of love to
you
Relax in His wings & be
comforted

Look into the Light & know His
path for you is Right.

Know you are His sweet child - He
Chose you for His great purpose

In my prayers
Love,
    Bambi
    7th

Introduction:

My child, you are not alone. I have never once taken My eyes off you. I cried the first tear when you heard those words, and I am no stranger to your pain. My heart breaks that you must embark on this unexpected journey. Right now, you face an important decision. You can travel through this dark valley alone, armed only with the world's weapons to fight against this cancer. Or, you can invite Me to go along with you and let Me light your way.

If you choose to invite Me into this journey, I promise to make My presence known to you. I will flood your heart with light so you can understand the wonderful future I have in store for you. My child, this cancer didn't come from Me and it was not My plan for your life. But if you take My hand, I promise to lead you to a place of intimacy with Me you have never known before—a place you could never go on your own power. With each step along the way, the pages in this book will give you a better understanding of who I am, whose you are, and all I can be for you during this journey.

Child, My love for you is endless and unfailing, and My Word is your best weapon against this enemy. In My kingdom where I rule and reign, there is no cancer and all things are possible. To make a way for you, I gave you a priceless gift. I gave up My rights as God and came to earth to share My message of hope and reveal My compassion for the sick and the lost. My child, I am a good God, and I have good plans for you. My will for your life is perfect, and I have given you a personal Savior, My Spirit, to guide you along the way. Through this journey, you must remember My power is not bound by worldly limitations. My grace made it possible for you to live with Me forever. In spite of your falls and failures, My tender mercies start fresh every day. Child, hear My gentle voice as we commune together in prayer, and experience My faithfulness as you trust in My promises. I will cover you with a peace that is not of this world and make you My righteousness. Yes, child, I am your Healer, and I am sovereign over your journey toward wholeness. As you wait for My perfect timing, you can find rest in the secret place of My presence where no evil can touch you. I will be your provider through this unexpected journey and show you My glory.

My child, take My hand. Come into the light and let Me lead you through this dark valley of cancer and all the twists and turns along the way. As you journey through each chapter of this book, open your heart and ponder My nature and who I am as I speak to you. With each scripture, proclaim My promises back to Me as you pray for the cure and everything else you so desperately need. When you reach the other side of the valley, I promise you will not be the same person who began this journey. You will be a reflection of Me. You will carry the same light that led you through the darkness, an irresistible light that will attract others into your glow.

My child, I am yours. I am your heavenly Father who created you, the Son who died for you, and the Holy Spirit who dwells within you. I am the Lord your God, and you are never alone. You are Mine forever.

Chapter 1: His Love

The Perfect Medicine

*And may you have the power to understand, as all God's people
should, how wide, how long, how high, and how deep his love is.
May you experience the love of Christ, though it is too great
to understand fully. Then you will be made complete with
all the fullness of life and power that comes from God.*
Ephesians 3:18–19

My child, you are embarking on an unexpected journey, one that
neither of us chose for you. It was never My plan that you should
be afflicted with sickness and disease. It was never My plan that you
should hear the words, "You have cancer." While you may be uncertain of what your future will bring, you can always be certain of My
love for you. In the midst of your uncertainty, your brokenness, and
your tattered emotions, I am with you.

Through it all, My child, I never once stopped loving you. I loved
you before you were ever conceived. I made all the delicate, inner
parts of your body, and I knit you together in your mother's womb
(Psalm 139:15–16). I was there at your birth to hear your first cry,
and I delighted in watching you grow into the beautiful person you
are today. I know everything about you and everything you do. I have
never taken my eyes off you. I know when you sit down or stand up,
I know your secret thoughts, and I know every word you say before
you say it. I am with you in all your comings and goings; I go before
you, and I follow you from behind (Psalm 139:2–5). Yes, My child,
I created you out of love, and I made you in My image. You are
perfectly and wonderfully made, My precious masterpiece (Genesis
1:27; Psalm 139:2–5, 13–16; Ephesians 2:10).

Beloved, I was there when you received the news. It breaks My
heart to think that cancer or any other setback would cause you

to doubt My love for you. To help you understand how wide, how long, how high, and how deep My love really is, imagine yourself standing on a beach with the sandy shoreline extending for miles and miles on each side. Now, reach down and scoop up a handful of sand and let the grains of sand slowly run through your fingers. Child, My thoughts about you far outnumber the grains of sand on the seashore of all the beaches in the world (Psalm 139:17–18)! Now gaze at the vast ocean in front of you and imagine My love stretching out as far as your eyes can see. My love is wide enough to cover your sorrows of today and long enough to cover your uncertain tomorrows. My love reaches up as high as the heavens are above the water and as deep as the ocean floor. It touches the heights of your good times and the depths of your despair. My love reaches the very root of the cancer that threatens to steal your hopes and dreams.

Dear one, it has always been My heart's desire to lavish My love on you, simply because you are Mine (1 John 3:1). My love for you knows no boundaries (Hosea 14:4). There is nothing you can do to earn it and nothing you can do to lose it. I proved the width, length, height, and depth of My love through My Son.

As you set out on this journey, may you experience My love, though it is too great to fully understand. Let it be the perfect medicine for your body and a soothing balm for your soul. Then you will be made complete with all the fullness of life and power that comes from Me.

PRAY

UNCHANGING LOVE

*Your unfailing love, O LORD, is as vast as the heavens;
your faithfulness reaches beyond the clouds. Your righteousness is
like the mighty mountains, your justice like the ocean depths.
You care for people and animals alike, O LORD.
How precious is your unfailing love, O God!*
PSALM 36:5–7

Lord, when evil plots against me, sometimes I forget that Your love is truly as vast as the heavens above. Thank You that Your faithfulness reaches beyond the clouds, that Your righteousness is as immovable as the mighty mountains, and that Your justice will prevail against the enemy who threatens to steal my destiny. As I walk through this valley of cancer, help me remember that Your precious love will uphold me through every decision, every treatment, and every challenge along the way. Thank You for an unchanging love that never fails, never runs out, and lasts forever.

INSEPARABLE LOVE

*And I am convinced that nothing can ever separate us from God's love.
Neither death nor life, neither angels nor demons, neither our fears for
today nor our worries about tomorrow—not even the powers of hell can
separate us from God's love. No power in the sky above or in the earth
below—indeed, nothing in all creation will ever be able to separate us
from the love of God that is revealed in Christ Jesus our Lord.*
ROMANS 8:38–39

Your love is completely unchanging, unconquerable, and unconditional, Father. There is nothing I could ever do to make You love me more, and nothing I could ever do to lose Your love. Hardship, persecution, or even a threat against my life is never a sign You have abandoned me or stopped loving me. No, it is virtually impossible for You to withhold

Your love from me. I praise You, Lord! There is nothing—not death or life, not angels or demons, not my fears for today or my worries about tomorrow, not the powers of hell, *not even cancer*—that can ever separate me from the love that You revealed for me through Christ Jesus!

Unfailing Love

O Lord, you are so good, so ready to forgive,
so full of unfailing love for all who ask for your help.
Psalm 86:5

I am in deep trouble! I never expected to find myself in this battle. In the back of my mind, I always thought cancer happens to other people. I'm so sorry if I haven't always shown Your compassion for others facing this disease. Please hear my cry for help! I am desperate, Lord. I need You. You are so good to me, so ready to forgive and show Your mercy. Thank You for the promise of Your unfailing, abounding love. I trust You, Lord. I trust You will answer my cries for help.

Everlasting Love

Long ago the Lord said to Israel: "I have loved
you, my people, with an everlasting love.
With unfailing love I have drawn you to myself."
Jeremiah 31:3

Lord, You were so kind and merciful to Israel, Your chosen people. When they turned their backs on You countless times to follow their sinful nature, You were always eager to help them and draw them back to Your heart. Forgive me when I have done the same thing, when I have turned my back on You to go my own way. Thank You for Your unfailing love that always draws me back to You and welcomes me home. Thank You for loving me with an everlasting love!

Sacrificial Love

But God showed his great love for us by sending Christ
to die for us while we were still sinners.
ROMANS 5:8

My human mind can't comprehend that You would come to earth as a humble baby to pay the price for my mistakes—that You would carry the sin of the entire world on Your back! I simply can't grasp a love so deep. Some say it wasn't necessary for the Romans soldiers to nail You to the cross because Your love would have held You there. Lord, thank You for Your sacrificial love. You suffered a criminal's death at Calvary, and You would have done it just for me. You were mocked, bloodied, and beaten beyond recognition, all so I could be healed and set free.

Real Love

God showed how much he loved us by sending his one and only Son
into the world so that we might have eternal life through him.
This is real love—not that we loved God, but that he loved
us and sent his Son as a sacrifice to take away our sins.
1 JOHN 4:9–11

God, You didn't just create me to inhabit the earth at this time and place in history. You created me in order to love me. You love me so much that You want to live with me forever. You want to spend all eternity with me. And You gave me the freedom to choose whether to accept Your offer. Lord, I accept! Thank You for loving me in spite of my brokenness. I'm sorry for my failures and shortcomings. Come into my life and into the midst of this cancer. Thank You that nothing I have ever done or could ever do is beyond Your outstretched arms of love. Thank You, Lord, for real love.

Merciful Love

But because of his great love for us, God, who is rich in mercy,
made us alive with Christ even when we were dead
in transgressions—it is by grace you have been saved.
And God raised us up with Christ and seated us with
him in the heavenly realms in Christ Jesus.
EPHESIANS 2:4–6 NIV

Thank You, Lord, for reaching Your nail-scarred hand into my darkness and raising me up from the dead and into the light. You not only saved me from a life of hopelessness and despair, but You united me with Christ and seated me with Him in the heavenly realms! Thank You for a love so great that I am made perfect in Your sight, because You see me through heaven's eyes. Because of Your great and merciful love, I am alive!

Lavish Love

See what great love the Father has lavished on us,
that we should be called children of God!
And that is what we are!
1 JOHN 3:1 NIV

Heavenly Father, when I think that You call me Your child, I am reminded of the great love earthly parents have for their children. Early in life, children are fully dependent on their parents for their every need. As toddlers, they stumble and make messes. As they grow older, their parents continue to nurture and love them despite their mistakes. How much more, Lord, do You lavish Your love on me? Even the best earthly parent isn't perfect, but You, Lord, are the perfect Father. Thank You that I am Your child, and You love me through all my stumbles, messes, and mistakes. Thank You for Your extravagant love that will carry me through this cancer.

Joyful Love

"For the LORD your God is living among you. He is a mighty savior.
He will take delight in you with gladness. With his love,
he will calm all your fears. He will rejoice
over you with joyful songs."
ZEPHANIAH 3:17

Lord, I am awestruck to think that the Creator of the entire universe delights in me so much that He sings joyful love songs over me! Thank You that You are not a disengaged Father who only loves me from a distance, but a mighty Savior who lives *with* me today—a Father who loves spending time with me, as a parent loves spending quality time with their child! Lord, thank You that Your powerful love calms all my fears. When I doubt Your love for me, help me to hear Your joyful songs!

Abiding Love

"I have loved you even as the Father has loved me. Remain in my
love. When you obey my commandments, you remain in my love,
just as I obey my Father's commandments and remain in his love."
JOHN 15:9–10

Jesus, thank You for loving me just as Your Father loved You. Even when I drift away from my fellowship with You, You always remain in a relationship with me. Lord, thank You for Your abiding love that never fails! Help me to remain in the grip of Your steadfast love and to obey You, just as You obeyed Your Father. When nothing makes sense as I travel through this dark valley, please keep me from pulling away from You. Help me to remain in Your love, just as You remained in His love in the face of persecution.

Agape Love

We know how much God loves us, and we have put our trust in his love. God is love, and all who live in love live in God, and God lives in them.
1 John 4:16

You do not merely love me, Father God. You are love itself. Thank You for *agape love*, a perfect, unconditional, and sacrificial love that is of You and from You alone. Love is Your very nature and drives all that You are and all that You do. Thank You that everything flows from Your agape love. If I have You in my life, I truly have everything I need. Lord, the only way I can respond to a love so sure and so complete is to place all my trust in You. Please help me to know You and fully depend on Your love as a little child trusts a loving parent. Help me to trust in Your love through every challenge this cancer brings.

Perfect Love

Such love has no fear, because perfect love expels all fear. If we are afraid, it is for fear of punishment, and this shows that we have not fully experienced his perfect love.
1 John 4:18

Lord, fear cannot coexist with Your perfect love. Thank You that I never have to live in fear of what my future might bring because You love me perfectly. I never have to fear condemnation and punishment because You took the punishment for me. Lord, please help me to fully experience Your perfect love! I know in my head that You love me. Please help me to know it in my heart. Help me to receive the fullness of Your love as I struggle with the reality of this diagnosis. Let Your perfect love expel my fear for today's tests, tomorrow's treatments, and all the future will bring.

Unconditional Love

*Jesus replied, "The most important commandment is this: 'Listen, O Israel!
The Lord our God is the one and only Lord. And you must love the Lord
your God with all your heart, all your soul, all your mind, and all your
strength.' The second is equally important: 'Love your neighbor
as yourself.' No other commandment is greater than these."*
MARK 12:29–31

I can love You only because You loved me first, God. You loved me
in spite of my faults and failures, and You suffered and died to prove
it. When I fully understand the scope of Your unconditional love for
me, I can't help but love You from a grateful heart. Lord, I can only
truly love myself if I believe that I am worthy of Your love. If there
is anything standing in the way of my receiving the fullness of Your
love, please show me! Thank You that I am made worthy by Your
blood, regardless of my past! I want to be all in, Lord. I want to love
You with all of me—my heart, my soul, my mind, and my strength.
Help me to love others as I am learning to love myself—with the
same unconditional, infinite love that You love me.

Enduring Love

*Give thanks to the God of heaven.
His faithful love endures forever.*
PSALM 136:26

You offer me the only love that is faithful and truly lasts forever.
Even the people who are closest to me, those who love me most
in this earthly life, will sometimes fail me and withhold their love
from me. But You, Lord, will never fail me. Your goodness, kindness,
compassion, and faithfulness will never run out. You loved me before
I was ever conceived, You will love me through all my days on this
earth, and You will love me throughout eternity. I give thanks to You,
Lord! Your faithful love endures forever.

Chapter 2: His Goodness

All the Time, I Am Good

❧

You are good and do only good; teach me your decrees.
PSALM 119:68

My child, I know you are wondering, "Why me?" "How did this happen?" Or even, "What did I do to deserve this?" As you ponder these questions, it grieves Me that you might think I am somehow the cause of this cancer. If you believe it's possible this illness came from Me, you might be tempted to push Me away in anger, or find it difficult to come to Me for healing and restoration. Even your past experiences with an earthly father or authority figure can distort your view of My goodness. I understand it can be difficult to trust Me if you think I'm mad at you or punishing you for something. It can be very difficult for you to come to Me for healing if you think your prayers might be contrary to My plans for you.

No beloved, I am a *good* God, and you belong to Me! You are My very own child. I am not a mean, cruel, and vindictive Father who makes people sick. From the very beginning, I have loved you with an unfailing, everlasting, and perfect love. It is not My nature or My purpose to cause you to suffer, but to give you a rich and satisfying life (John 10:10)! When I was here on earth, I didn't go around inflicting people with disease and calamity. On the contrary, I went around doing good! I healed and delivered every person who came to Me (Acts 10:36–38).

I understand how a serious diagnosis like cancer can tempt even My strongest, faith-filled child to doubt My goodness. But there is another whose purpose is to steal, kill, and destroy (John 10:10). He prowls around like a roaring lion, looking for someone to devour

(1 Peter 5:8–9). If it steals, kills, and destroys, you can be certain it's not Me. Satan is behind the evil in this world and any sickness that threatens to destroy My children. That's why Peter warns you to stay alert and strong in your faith (1 Peter 5:8) and Paul tells you to be strong in My power so you can stand firm against Satan's strategies and tricks (Ephesians 6:11). One of his tricks is to distract your attention away from Me and cause you to doubt My goodness (Mark 4:14–19).

Yes, My child, it is true that I can use your suffering for My glory and purposes (Romans 8:28). I can take everything the enemy is intending for destruction and use it for your good. But I did not make you sick, and it is not My plan that you should suffer! I am not the author of sickness and disease. When you are tempted to doubt My love and goodness, think about this: If you are a parent, would you ever strike your own children with a devastating disease and then abandon them in the middle of nowhere as a punishment for their misbehavior? Is it in your nature to do such a thing? If your own children asked you for a loaf of bread, would you give them a stone instead? If they asked you for a fish, would you give them a snake? If you, as a sinful and fallible people, know how to give good gifts to your children, then how much more will I, your heavenly Father, give to you (Matthew 7:9–11)? My child, it is not My nature to be cruel, vindictive, or indifferent. I am a good Father who loves and cares for you, infinitely more so than the best earthly parent. I am good, and I do only good. All the time, I am good.

PRAY

GOODNESS FOR ALL

The LORD is good to everyone.
He showers compassion on all his creation.
PSALM 145:9

Your goodness is for *all* creation. Your sun shines on both evil and good alike, and Your rain falls on both the just and the unjust. As I walk through this valley of cancer, thank You that Your compassion and care for me is not dependent on my own goodness, but on Your goodness alone. I am Your creation, and You promise to shower compassion on all Your creation. Thank You for being a good God to everyone.

GOODNESS IN ALL

Then God looked over all he had made,
and he saw that it was very good!
GENESIS 1:31

Creator God, everything You made is very good—excellent in every way! Because I am part of Your creation, I, too, am excellent in every way. You are pleased with how You made me, Lord! Because cancer is not good, You did not create it, and because You made me excellent in every way, You did not create me to be afflicted with cancer. Therefore, in Your precious name, I command my body to come back into agreement with the goodness of Your creation. Thank You, Lord!

He Created Good

Since everything God created is good,
we should not reject any of it but receive it with thanks.
1 Timothy 4:4

Heavenly Father, I know everything You created is good, but right now I feel as if I have been betrayed by my own body! I trusted my body would hold up through the wear and tear of living and give me a long life. Please Lord, forgive me if I have ever taken Your gift of health for granted. Lord, every gift I receive from You is good. I thank You and praise You for all these gifts, especially a lifetime of health and wellness. Help me to always use my gifts and blessings to serve You and bring You glory.

His Lasting Goodness

Give thanks to the Lord, for he is good!
His faithful love endures forever.
Psalm 107:1

Just as Your love endures forever, Lord, so Your goodness lasts forever. I can't keep this good news to myself. I give thanks to You, Lord! You have done so much for me! Thank You for family, friends, and provision. Thank You for health and wholeness. If my life on earth ended today and I was swept up on the wings of heaven, I have had a rich and full life. Thank You, Lord. Thank You for all my blessings. Thank You for life itself.

Gifts from Heaven

*Whatever is good and perfect is a gift coming down to us
from God our Father, who created all the lights in the heavens.
He never changes or casts a shifting shadow.*
James 1:17

Lord, You are the source of everything good in my life. You are the Light of the world, the Light of heaven that came to penetrate into the darkness! You never change and never cast a shifting shadow. Lord, light cannot coexist with darkness. Please shine Your light into this cancer that lurks in the dark and hidden places of my body! Shine Your goodness into this disease. Expose it and replace it with Your glorious light! I trust You, Lord. Thank You for healing and restoring me in whatever way You choose to heal. Thank You for your good and perfect gifts.

Goodness for Now

*Yet I am confident I will see the Lord's goodness
while I am here in the land of the living.*
Psalm 27:13

Father, I'm so grateful that I don't have to wait for heaven to see Your goodness. You came to earth so I could have a rich and satisfying life beginning right here and now on this side of eternity. Lord, You have been so good to me! Help me be confident of this amazing promise, that I will always see Your goodness in the land of the living. Please show me Your goodness through this cancer journey.

Taste His Goodness

Taste and see that the LORD is good.
Oh, the joys of those who take refuge in him!
PSALM 34:8

Lord, You challenge me to taste and see that You are good—to believe in You and see for myself that You are a good God. I want to taste and see, Lord! Help me to take the first step of faith through this unexpected journey. Help me to trust in You tomorrow, the next day, and the next. You are my refuge! I want to taste Your goodness, Lord. There is no joy in cancer, but I want to experience Your joy in spite of it.

⌒

Only God

Someone came to Jesus with this question: "Teacher, what good deed must I do to have eternal life?" "Why ask me about what is good?" Jesus replied. "There is only One who is good. But to answer your question—if you want to receive eternal life, keep the commandments."
MATTHEW 19:16–17

This rich man asked what good things he could do to earn eternal life. But Lord, only You are good. I can't offer You a list of the good things I have done to earn Your favor. You would not accept my offer. All You ask me to do is to put You first in my life. Forgive me for the modern-day idols of my heart that have replaced You. Forgive me for holding on too tightly to the temporal things of this world that I can touch and see. You alone are worthy of my praise. You alone are good. I am saved and healed by Your goodness alone.

No Good Thing Withheld

For the LORD God is our sun and our shield. He gives us grace
and glory. The LORD will withhold no good thing
from those who do what is right.
PSALM 84:11

Lord, Your grace and glory are overwhelming! While You may not always give me everything I want, I know You will always provide everything I need. I know You will withhold no good thing from me. Lord, today I need Your strength! I need Your hope for tomorrow! There is a very dark valley ahead of me and darkness surrounds me. I will walk through it, Lord, but I can't do it without You. Hold nothing back, Lord! Thank You for being my sun and my shield.

Storehouse of Goodness

How great is the goodness you have stored up for those
who fear you. You lavish it on those who come to you
for protection, blessing them before the watching world.
PSALM 31:19

Father, I come to You for protection, and I am expectant! You are not a God of scarcity and limitation, but a God of abundance. There is more than enough of Your goodness to go around! Lord, because You are good, I can expect good things. I don't have to be like a window shopper, wistfully longing to have the good things I see on the other side of the glass. How great is Your goodness, Lord! You have a storehouse in heaven with my name on it! Lavish Your blessing on me before the watching world so I can be a testimony of Your goodness.

Good Plans

*"For I know the plans I have for you," says the L*ORD.
"They are plans for good and not for disaster,
to give you a future and a hope."
JEREMIAH 29:11

I take great comfort in knowing that You have already planned my future, and Your plans for me are good and full of hope, Lord. You created me with a purpose, and You will walk alongside me all the days of my life as my purpose unfolds. Lord, while You have promised me a rich and satisfying life, I know that my days won't always be void of hardship, suffering, and pain. But from beginning to end, I trust You will see me through to a glorious conclusion because You are good and Your plans are good. Thank You that my story has a perfect ending.

Goodness in All Circumstances

And we know that God causes everything to work together for the good
of those who love God and are called according to his purpose for them.
ROMANS 8:28

God, I know this cancer did not come from You. It is the enemy's purpose to steal, kill, and destroy, not Yours. But I still struggle with the question of why. I understand there are some things I will never know until I meet You face-to-face on the day of glory. In the meantime, please help me to surrender all my questions. Help me to be content not knowing all the answers, but to just know You, Lord. You are enough! I know You are working to fulfill Your purpose in my life. Thank You for Your promise to use everything—the victories and disappointments, the good and the bad, even this cancer—for Your good purposes. Help me to trust You to bring long-term good out of this cancer, to use what the enemy intended for evil for Your good and for Your glory.

His Goodness Revealed

*The LORD replied, "I will make all my goodness pass before you,
and I will call out my name, Yahweh, before you."*
EXODUS 33:19

My life is a whirlwind of activity right now, Father. Appointments, tests, and phone calls fill my days while a flood of treatment options and decisions fill my mind at night. Thank You that through it all, You promise to make Your goodness pass before me. Lord, I want to see You clearly in the midst of all the turmoil. I want to hear Your voice above all the noise. Guide me, Lord. Help me to see You in every detail. Nothing happening around me is coincidental. Thank You for Your presence and Your wisdom in my midst. Show me Your glory, Lord! Reveal Your goodness!

His Goodness Assured

*Surely your goodness and unfailing love will pursue me all the days
of my life, and I will live in the house of the LORD forever.*
PSALM 23:6

Father God, You are the perfect Shepherd. All the times I wandered away, got lost or stuck, stumbled, questioned, or resisted Your goodness, You never once stopped loving me. You never once stopped pursuing me. Even when I walk through the dark valley of cancer, I will have no fear because You walk with me. You look out for me and protect me in the presence of my enemy. Lord, thank You for the eternal promise that Your goodness and unfailing love will pursue me all the days of my life. I will live forever in Your house.

Chapter 3: His Word

Inspired by God

*All Scripture is inspired by God and is useful to teach us what is true
and to make us realize what is wrong in our lives. It corrects us when
we are wrong and teaches us to do what is right. God uses it to
prepare and equip his people to do every good work.*
2 Timothy 3:16–17

My child, your Bible is more than a collection of stories. Your Bible
is My Word, and My Word is truth. Through My Spirit, I revealed
Myself to faithful ones who wrote down My message from their
own historical and cultural contexts. They wrote what I inspired
them to write, so when you study the Scriptures, you can make it
your standard for testing everything else around you that claims to
be true. My Word is a lamp unto your feet and your guiding light
for how to live (Psalm 119:105). There is not one feeling or emotion,
from fear and hopelessness to glorious victory, not one situation you
will encounter in this journey through cancer that My Word does
not touch. It speaks to the depths of your suffering and brings comfort in the midst of your deepest sorrow. Yes, child, My Word is full
of living power (Hebrews 4:12). You can do anything My Word says
you can do, you can be anything it says you can be, and you can have
anything it says you can have!

Dear one, I AM my Word. I existed before the world began. I
created everything there is. And then I came in human form to live
on earth among you (John 11:1–3, 14). I am the Word, and I meet
every human need. I came to heal you and save you from destruction
(Psalm 107:20). When you battle this cancer, you can easily focus
on your circumstances: the symptoms, doctors, tests, medications,
and prognoses. You can take your eyes off Me, the ultimate Healer

and the only one who can calm the storm. When my servant Peter walked on water, he shared My power over the natural realm as long as he looked into the eyes of Truth. He only panicked and sunk because he took his eyes off Me and focused on his circumstances. He began depending on His own strength and became aware of his own limitations (Matthew 14:22–33).

There are times, beloved, when facts around you don't agree with the truth of My Word. It may be an undeniable fact that you have been diagnosed with cancer. The truth is, you have been healed by My wounds (1 Peter 2:24). It may be a fact that the cancer is aggressive. The truth is, nothing is impossible for Me (Luke 1:37). It may be a fact that there is no cure. The truth is, everyone who keeps on asking will be given what they ask for (Luke 11:9–11). It may be a fact that cancer can limit life expectancy. But the truth is, I will satisfy you with a long life (Psalm 91:15–16).

My child, please don't let your experiences cause you to doubt My truth. Never assume that I won't heal, simply because your circumstances look dismal or you know someone who prayed and didn't get well. I am your standard for all truth, not your experience. While here on earth, I healed everyone who came to Me. In My unlimited power, it's possible to transcend the facts like Peter did. In My presence, there can be peace instead of fear when the storms rage around you. Even when you start to sink, it is impossible for Me to let you drown. My Word promises to give you back your health and heal your wounds (Jeremiah 30:17). By My tender mercies, I healed all your diseases (Psalm 103:2–3). My eternal truth always triumphs. My child, will you come into agreement with Me?

PRAY

Absolute Truth

All your words are true;
all your righteous laws are eternal.
PSALM 119:160 NIV

Lord, Your very character is truthfulness. You are the perfect Father, and it is completely against your nature to lie. Lord, Your truth is my plumb line, the standard for testing everything else around me that claims to be true. Thank You that I can always trust Your Word is true and dependable. Help me not to waver when the voices of the world contradict Your truth. Lord, Your truth is absolute. Your truth is perfect. All Your words are true!

His Word Stands

"The grass withers and the flowers fade,
but the word of our God stands forever."
ISAIAH 40:8

Father, Your Word is the final authority and the lasting solution to every problem I will ever encounter. In the midst of a dying and decaying world inhabited by mere mortals, Your Word is eternal and unfailing. Science and technology will always make new discoveries. Medical opinions may differ and treatment options may advance and change. But You, Lord, never change. Your Word is constant. Your Word stands the test of time. Thank You that Your Word stands forever.

His Healing Word

But the officer said, "Lord, I am not worthy to have you come into my home. Just say the word from where you are, and my servant will be healed."
MATTHEW 8:8

You are Jehovah-Rapha, the God who heals. When You walked on this earth, You only spoke, and all the sick people who came to You were healed by the power and authority of Your word. This Roman officer knew You could just give the command and his servant would be healed without You even coming to his home. You were so amazed by his faith, You healed his servant that very hour! Lord, Your word has power and authority over this cancer! Say the word so I will be healed.

Living Word

So the Word became human and made his home among us. He was full of unfailing love and faithfulness. And we have seen his glory, the glory of the Father's one and only Son.
JOHN 1:14

Lord, You are the Word. You existed before the world began. You created everything there is, and then You came in human form to make Your home with me. You are the foundation for all truth, the truth itself made flesh. Lord, while here on earth, You demonstrated Your truth. You showed me how to live, and You demonstrated Your unfailing love and faithfulness. You are the living example of Your Word, the perfect reality of all Your promises. Forgive me for ever doubting Your passion and Your power to heal. Show me Your glory, Lord!

Sustaining Word

The Son is the radiance of God's glory and the exact representation
of his being, sustaining all things by his powerful word.
After he had provided purification for sins, he sat down
at the right hand of the Majesty in heaven.
HEBREWS 1:3 NIV

According to the scripture, God, You merely spoke Your Word and the entire world appeared at Your command! The radiance of Your glory gives life and sustains all things by Your powerful Word. Lord, I am humbled and amazed to know that the same power that created the universe and placed the stars in the sky cleanses my sin and sustains my very life. Yes, Lord, in You I live and breathe and have my very existence. Your work is complete, Lord. Thank You that I am complete in You.

Truth Brings Freedom

To the Jews who had believed him, Jesus said, "If you hold
to my teaching, you are really my disciples. Then you will
know the truth, and the truth will set you free."
JOHN 8:31–32 NIV

Thank You, Father, that Your Word is the perfect standard for what is right and true. Help me, Lord! This cancer is holding me captive in the enemy's grip. I know his only purpose is to steal, kill, and destroy. But Your Word frees me from his grip, and all the consequences of sin and death. Help me hold on to Your Word, Lord. Help me hold on to Your truth. Your Word restores me. Your truth will set me free!

Made Holy

Make them holy by your truth;
teach them your word, which is truth.
JOHN 17:17

Lord, thank You that I am saved for all eternity by accepting Your forgiveness through Your sacrifice on the cross! But I want more, Lord. I want to be made pure and holy by Your truth. Teach me Your Word, Lord. Your Word is the only truth. Help me to believe and obey Your Word. Purify my mind and my heart as I follow Your path in my daily life. Continue to purify me as I walk through this valley.

Guiding Light

Your commandments give me understanding;
no wonder I hate every false way of life. Your word is
a lamp to guide my feet and a light for my path.
PSALM 119:104–105

As I walk through the dark valley of cancer, thank You that Your Word lights my way. Guide me, Father, and keep me from stumbling. Throughout this journey, please protect me from deceitful philosophies, false gods, false religions, or anything else I may encounter along the way that is not of You and does not align with Your perfect truth. Lord, please give me Your wisdom and discernment. Help me to know Your Word so I am not led astray. Thank You for being my guiding light.

True Life

*But Jesus told him, "No! The Scriptures say,
'People do not live by bread alone, but by every
word that comes from the mouth of God.'"*
MATTHEW 4:4

Jesus, when You were here on earth You were fully human and fully divine. But You put Your deity aside to share in my humanness and show me how to live in Your mighty power, the life You intended me to live. Lord, You are no stranger to my pain. Even though You were hungry, weak, and tormented by evil, You were victorious over sin and death. Forgive me when I forget that only You can satisfy my deepest longings. The world will never satisfy and give me the good life I crave. Only You can satisfy. I don't live by bread alone, but by every powerful word that comes from Your mouth. Your Word gives me true life.

Alive and Powerful

*For the word of God is alive and powerful. It is sharper
than the sharpest two-edged sword, cutting between soul
and spirit, between joint and marrow. It exposes our
innermost thoughts and desires.*
HEBREWS 4:12

Lord, nothing is hidden from You. Your Word exposes everything about me. It reveals who I am, and who You called me to be. It penetrates into the depths of my spirit and soul, exposing my innermost thoughts and desires. Your Word is living, life changing, and dynamic, continuously refining me and leading me on the path toward my destiny. Lord, as I walk this path through cancer, help me to respond to Your Word in a way that honors You and brings You glory. By the power of Your Word, help me to live the life You created me to live.

THE SOURCE OF WISDOM

"Anyone who listens to my teaching and follows it is wise,
like a person who builds a house on solid rock."
MATTHEW 7:24

God, help me to be wise. I want to build my life on a solid foundation. I want to listen to Your teaching and follow it so I can put it into daily practice. Give me a hunger for Your Word! Draw me deeply into Your truth. Help me be so immersed in Your Word that I cannot be shaken when a storm like cancer comes into my life. Lord, all Your promises are true. I want Your Word to be permanently etched on my heart. Even if I don't have a Bible in front of me, I want to be able to draw on Your specific promises at the time of testing. Help me build my life on You, Lord. You are my solid rock.

FAITH BY HEARING

So then faith comes by hearing,
and hearing by the word of God.
ROMANS 10:17 NKJV

Lord, in this time of deep testing, increase my faith! Lead me to a church where I can hear Your truth being preached with boldness. Lead me to conferences and prayer meetings where the power of Your healing Word is believed and demonstrated. Lead me to teaching CDs and sacred music that will fill my home with the truth of scripture. Lord, by the power of Your spoken Word, help me to focus on Your truth and not this cancer. I want to know You, Lord. I want to know Your Word.

Never Empty

*It is the same with my word. I send it out, and it always
produces fruit. It will accomplish all I want it to,
and it will prosper everywhere I send it.*
ISAIAH 55:11

Father, You promise that Your Word always produces fruit. When
You send it out, it always accomplishes Your purposes. It never
comes back empty. Lord, lead me to Your truth in the scriptures
that specifically hold Your promises for me right now in my current
battle. I send out Your Word, Lord. I speak Your healing promises
out loud. No weapon formed against me will prosper! I have been
healed by Your stripes! I believe Your Word, Lord. I stand on Your
Word in faith. May the fruit of Your Word bring glory to Your name!

Fighting Words

*Put on salvation as your helmet,
and take the sword of the Spirit, which is the word of God.*
EPHESIANS 6:17

Lord, I am steeped in a battle You have already won. Nevertheless,
You are calling on me to fight back the darkness and contend for
the victory. Lord, I put on Your armor. I wear Your belt of truth to
discern the enemy's lies and Your body armor of righteousness that
ensures Your love for me. I wear Your shoes of peace to give me
courage and carry Your shield of faith to protect me from all the fiery
arrows the enemy launches against me. Your helmet of salvation protects my mind from doubting Your promises. But Lord, the sword is
Your Word! It is my only offensive weapon against the enemy and
the very same weapon You used against him in the wilderness. Lord,
help me fight back with Your Word. Thank You for your truth that
triumphs over all the facts raging around me!

Chapter 4: His Kingdom

The Kingdom Is Near!

◆

"The time promised by God has come at last!" he announced.
"The Kingdom of God is near! Repent of your sins
and believe the Good News!"

MARK 1:15

My child, it was always My intention to have an intimate relationship with you. It broke My heart when My first children disobeyed Me and gave in to the Tempter. Their mistake ushered sin and destruction into the paradise I created for them and destroyed our intimacy. From that point on, generations of My people repeatedly turned their hearts away from Me to follow their sinful ways even though I extended My mercy countless times. Even then, I had a perfect plan to make sure the darkness wouldn't last forever. I made a promise through My prophet Isaiah that, "the people who walk in darkness will see a great Light" (Isaiah 9:2). I promised over three hundred times through My prophets in the Old Testament that I would come to save you! For centuries, My people waited for the anointed One who would rescue them from their oppressors and establish My new kingdom on earth.

Finally, two thousand years ago, I came to take back what the enemy stole from you in the garden. By the time My promise came to pass, My people were hopelessly oppressed by the Roman Empire. But I came to break the power of sin, to set things right again, and to initiate My kingdom on earth (Matthew 12:28; Luke 4:18–20). I came to give life in all its fullness, to comfort the brokenhearted, and to set the captives free (John 10:10; Isaiah 61:1). I shared the Good News of My kingdom everywhere I went by teaching, preaching, and healing people of every kind of disease and sickness (Mark

4:23). I wanted you to understand that My kingdom is not just a place you can hope to experience in the future, but a realm of power making *all* things possible today. In My kingdom, under My divine rule and reign and by the power of My Spirit, there is intimacy, love, goodness, peace, joy, healing, and abundant life. My kingdom is free from pain, suffering, hatred, and evil. The Light of the world can never be overcome with darkness (John 1:4).

Yes, beloved, there is still evil in the world. You will have many trials and sorrows on earth, maybe even cancer. But take heart, because I have overcome the world (John 16:33)! Through My resurrection, I provided the full measure of grace to restore all things (Colossians 1:20), and I will continue My work until it is finally finished on the day when I return (Philippians 1:6). Until then, I am with you, just as I was with My children in the garden. You have My Spirit inside you as a foretaste of future glory—a time when I will completely free the world of all sin, sickness, and evil (Romans 8:19–23). During this interim time when My kingdom is here but not fully here, I established My Church to pour out My healing grace until My kingdom is complete.

My child, I have blessed you with intelligence and free will. Please don't grow too comfortable and dependent on a world of things you can touch, see, hear, and control. Can you not see it? My kingdom is near! You are not a child of this world, but a child of My kingdom where My power is unlimited. In My kingdom, you have been healed.

PRAY

Everlasting Kingdom

For your kingdom is an everlasting kingdom. You rule throughout all generations. The LORD always keeps his promises; he is gracious in all he does.
Psalm 145:13

Lord, I live in a world where things around me change every day—the latest in science, technology, social customs, and cultural values are all here today but gone tomorrow. But You, Lord, are my one constant. You never change! Thank You that You rule and reign throughout all generations and Your kingdom lasts forever. Forgive me for taking my eyes off You and forgetting Your promises. It's so easy to put my trust in the things I can touch, see, hear, and control instead of the realm of things unseen. Thank You for grace! I am not a child of the world, but a child of Your everlasting kingdom!

Indestructible Kingdom

"During the reigns of those kings, the God of heaven will set up a kingdom that will never be destroyed or conquered. It will crush all these kingdoms into nothingness, and it will stand forever."
Daniel 2:44

It is not world leaders, not the world's best doctors or scientists, nor the world's most brilliant people who will decide the outcome of history. Only You, God, have power, authority, and sovereignty over all human knowledge and all worldly kingdoms. You have the final authority over this cancer, Lord. Thank You that your rule is eternal and Your kingdom is indestructible! As a child of the kingdom, I am secure in You. I am protected. I can never be destroyed or conquered!

His Perfect Plan

And this is the plan: At the right time he will bring
everything together under the authority
of Christ—everything in heaven and on earth.
Ephesians 1:10

Lord, sometimes I don't understand Your plans. And even when I think I understand Your plans, I don't understand Your timing! Help me to trust You, Lord. At the right time, You *will* bring all your creation together to be with You forever. Thank You for Your Church, the body of believers united as one under Your headship and authority. May Your kingdom advance until it is completely restored as it was in the beginning! I long for the complete coming of Your kingdom when You will rule over everything in heaven and earth, when every knee will bow to Your glorious name, and when all evil will be destroyed forever! Come, Lord Jesus!

As It Is in Heaven

Your kingdom come.
Your will be done on earth as it is in heaven.
Matthew 6:10 nkjv

Father, thank You for coming in the flesh to initiate Your rule and reign on earth! Lord, You have come to break the power of sin, heal the sick, and set the captives free at last! As I ponder the prayer You taught us to pray, I thank You that the coming of Your kingdom made all things possible now, including my complete healing and restoration. Lord, cancer is evil, so there can be no cancer in heaven. If there is no cancer in heaven, it cannot exist here! Lord, today I boldly call Your kingdom to earth! May Your kingdom come! May Your will be done here, in my body, as it is in heaven.

Seek Him First

Seek the Kingdom of God above all else, and live righteously,
and he will give you everything you need.
MATTHEW 6:33

Help me to seek You above all else, Father, and to put You first and foremost in my life! Please fill my thoughts with You and Your desires and help me to live as You lived. Please forgive me when I allow the distractions of the world, including this illness, to push You out of my life. I'm sorry for the times I have pursued the things I want and need, instead of relentlessly pursuing You. Lord, You are the Creator, the source of all my blessings, including the healing and restoration I desperately seek. Help me to seek Your kingdom *first*, and to trust You will provide *everything* else I need.

⁓

The Narrow Gate

"You can enter God's Kingdom only through the narrow gate.
The highway to hell is broad, and its gate is wide for the many
who choose that way. But the gateway to life is very narrow
and the road is difficult, and only a few ever find it."
MATTHEW 7:13–14

Lord, going to church and calling myself a Christian is the easy part. It's not so easy to follow You and to be obedient to Your plans and purposes when I have plans of my own! Forgive me, Lord. I want to be a true disciple. I want my heart's desires to be Yours. I want to know You. You are the only way to the kingdom, Lord. The gate may be narrow, but Your grace is wide and deep. Thank You that all who know You as Lord and Savior can enter, regardless of their past! Lord, I choose the narrow gate. I choose You. Be with me as I walk this difficult road. Help me to find the true gateway to life.

Keys of the Kingdom

"And I will give you the keys of the Kingdom of Heaven.
Whatever you forbid on earth will be forbidden in heaven,
and whatever you permit on earth will be permitted in heaven."
MATTHEW 16:19

Thank You for the keys that give me access to Your presence and Your promises today! Thank You that what I forbid here has already been forbidden in heaven, and what I permit here has already been permitted in heaven. In Your name, Lord, I forbid this cancer from inhabiting my body! It has no kingdom authority to exist here. In Your name, Lord, I permit Your healing presence, power, and promises to rule and reign over my life.

Kingdom Living

For the Kingdom of God is not just a lot of talk;
it is living by God's power.
1 CORINTHIANS 4:20

Lord, this verse tells me there is so much more to Your kingdom than just going to church on Sunday and knowing all the right Bible verses and the right words to say. Lord, I want my life to be more than just a lot of talk about You! I want to know You, Lord. I want to fully experience You and Your kingdom. I want to live by Your power, and I don't want to miss out on anything You have in store for me right here in this life! Lord, please teach me how to live and experience Your kingdom each and every day. Let my life be a reflection of Your power and glory!

Fight for It

From the days of John the Baptist until now the kingdom of heaven suffers violent assault, and violent men seize it by force [as a precious prize].
MATTHEW 11:12 AMP

Father, Your kingdom is like a precious prize worth fighting for. The enemy wants to steal my destiny and divert my attention away from You. Right now, he is trying to steal my health and wellness. Help me to lay hold of Your kingdom promises with ardent zeal and fight back the world's distractions. Lord, I want all Your kingdom promises, and I want to live a kingdom life. Please give me the endurance, courage, and unwavering faith I need to win the prize! Help me to fight for it!

The Kingdom within You

Now when He was asked by the Pharisees when the kingdom of God would come, He answered them and said, "The kingdom of God does not come with observation; nor will they say, 'See here!' or 'See there!' For indeed, the kingdom of God is within you."
LUKE 17:20–21 NKJV

When Your kingdom came to earth, Father, the people expected a tangible kingdom they could observe with their eyes. But You said the kingdom of God is within me! Lord, I can't even grasp that the very realm of power where You rule and reign—where there is love, goodness, peace, joy, healing, and abundant life—actually dwells within me! Lord, help me to fully understand the power and the promise of hope that I carry in my heart! By the Spirit's power, let Your kingdom fully manifest in my life and my relationships.

Not an Earthly Kingdom

Jesus answered, "My Kingdom is not an earthly kingdom.
If it were, my followers would fight to keep me from being handed
over to the Jewish leaders. But my Kingdom is not of this world."
JOHN 18:36

Lord, Your kingdom is not an earthly kingdom with geographic boundaries. Nor is it captured in a building or a human institution offering religious programs or events, or even a clinic filled with wise doctors, medicines, and promising treatments. As I get caught up in waging the worldly battle against this cancer, help me to hold on loosely to the things I can touch, see, hear, and control. Help me to trust You, Lord. The world's power is limited, but Your power is unlimited. In You, nothing is impossible. Your kingdom is not of this world.

Like a Child

But Jesus said, "Let the children come to me. Don't stop them!
For the Kingdom of Heaven belongs to those
who are like these children."
MATTHEW 19:14

Father God, as I ponder what small children are like, I am reminded that they are fully dependent on their parents for every need. They trust their parents to feed, clothe, and nurture them. They expect to be cared for and never spend a moment worrying about whether their parents will come through for them. They haven't lived long enough to allow their education, experience, or sophistication to stand in the way of simple faith. Lord, if the kingdom of heaven belongs to children, then please help me be more like a child!

HIDDEN TREASURE

*"The Kingdom of Heaven is like a treasure that a man discovered
hidden in a field. In his excitement, he hid it again and sold
everything he owned to get enough money to buy the field."*
MATTHEW 13:44

Lord, You compared your kingdom to a treasure a man discovered
hidden in a field. He sold everything he had to get enough money to
buy the field where the treasure was hidden. He was willing to give up
everything to obtain it. Lord, help me to know that Your kingdom is
more valuable than anything I could ever own or anything I could ever
want. In my desperate search for healing, help me to know Your kingdom is the greatest treasure I could ever obtain. You are the answer
to every problem I will ever encounter on this earth, including this
cancer. I am seeking Your kingdom, Lord. Help me to find it.

A MUSTARD SEED

*Jesus said, "How can I describe the Kingdom of God? What story should
I use to illustrate it? It is like a mustard seed planted in the ground.
It is the smallest of all seeds, but it becomes the largest of all garden
plants; it grows long branches, and birds can make nests in its shade."*
MARK 4:30–32

You compared the kingdom to a mustard seed, Father, the smallest
of all seeds a farmer can plant. Like a mustard seed, Your kingdom
has small beginnings but will grow to produce great results! Just as
birds can make nests in the shade of the mustard tree, thank You
that I can make my home in the protective shade of Your kingdom.
Thank You that I am not alone on this faith journey, nor am I facing
this cancer alone. I am part of a growing community of Your followers. My faith joined with theirs can accomplish great things for Your
kingdom. Please lead me to other believers who will come alongside
me in this quest for healing.

Chapter 5: His Gift

Too Wonderful for Words

❧

Thank God for this gift too wonderful for words!
2 CORINTHIANS 9:15

My child, it might surprise you to know that I'm not sitting up in heaven keeping track of your mistakes and planning your punishment, nor am I counting all your good deeds and handing out rewards. You simply can't earn your way into My favor. It's not about what you do. How will you ever know when you've done enough or been good enough? It's all about what I've done for you. I have given you a gift too wonderful for words. Of all My blessings, this gift is far greater than all the others. Before I gave you this perfect gift, you were held captive to a law you could never follow. You were a prisoner to your sin with no hope of escape. But in My mercy, I orchestrated the perfect escape plan to redeem you from the sin that had come into the world through one man in the garden (Romans 5:12). I came to earth to set you free.

Yes, I am the same God who created the heavens and earth, the same God who set the stars in place and called them by name. But I loved you so much, I couldn't bear watching you suffer. So I came to take the punishment for you once and for all. I came to exchange My righteousness for your sin. I came to earth as a humble baby, giving up My rights as God and making Myself as nothing (Philippians 2:6–7). When I walked the earth as a man, I healed the sick, fulfilling the word of the prophet Isaiah, who said, "He took our sicknesses and removed our diseases" (Matthew 8:17).

And then I suffered and died on a cross. I died, because you could never do enough. Because you are human, you can't possibly follow all the rules. No one can (Romans 3:20, 23). Before I came,

My people learned this lesson over and over. You can only be made right in My sight by trusting Me to take away your sins (Romans 3:22–23). In this one ultimate act of love, I paid your debt in full (Romans 3:24).

Beloved, you don't deserve this cancer. But no good deed would have prevented it. No amount of personal achievement or personal goodness will ever bridge the gap between your human imperfection and My perfection. Only by trusting what I did for you on the cross will you be whole and perfect in My sight (Ephesians 2:8–10). It doesn't matter who you are or what you have done. It is only by My grace that you receive My free gift of eternal life (Romans 3:20–25; John 3:16). My precious gift promises an eternal home where sorrow and mourning will disappear—a place where all the faithful will be reunited and sing songs of everlasting joy and gladness (Isaiah 35:10). You have been born into My family, and your slate is wiped clean! Whatever trial you face on this earth, you have a priceless inheritance that can never be destroyed (1 Peter 1:3–6)!

My child, when they whipped Me, you were healed. When I dragged the cross up the hill to Calvary, I carried the weight of your cancer on My back (2 Peter 2:24). When they nailed Me to the cross, I defeated your cancer and carried it with Me to the grave. I died to save the world, but I would have done it just for you. Have you accepted My gift?

PRAY

WE ALL FALL SHORT

For everyone has sinned;
we all fall short of God's glorious standard.
ROMANS 3:23

Lord, sometimes I think my mistakes are worse than those of other people I know, while other times, I think I'm doing fairly well by comparison. But You make it clear, Lord—sin is sin. We are human and we all make mistakes. It's in our nature to fall short of Your glorious standard. All sin, no matter how big or how small, cuts me off from fellowship with You, and all sin eventually leads to death. Thank You, Lord, that by Your death and resurrection, all sin can be forgiven and forgotten, once and for all!

FREE GIFT

For the wages of sin is death, but the free gift of God
is eternal life through Christ Jesus our Lord.
ROMANS 6:23

Lord, You are such a gentleman! You don't barge into my life and force me to believe a certain way or behave a certain way. You offer me the free gift of eternal life and give me the freedom to choose to receive it. Thank You, Lord, that by choosing You, I can have the gift of new life that begins on earth and continues forever! I can't begin to understand how much this love offering truly cost You.

Sin Offering

*For God made Christ, who never sinned, to be the
offering for our sin, so that we could be made
right with God through Christ.*
2 Corinthians 5:21

Jesus, it amazes me that You were a man who never sinned; yet You loved Your creation so much You were willing to take the sin of the entire world on Your back. At the cross, You took every sin ever committed and every sin that will ever be committed and atoned for it once and for all. In this "great exchange," You traded something of immeasurable worth for something entirely worthless. I can scarcely take it in, Lord. You traded Your righteousness for my sin! It humbles me that You made me right in Your eyes. Thank You, Lord, that when You look at me, You see the perfect, flawless child You created me to be.

The Way to Eternal Life

*"For this is how God loved the world: He gave his one and only Son,
so that everyone who believes in him will not perish but have eternal
life. God sent his Son into the world not to judge the world,
but to save the world through him."*
John 3:16–17

Father, You paid dearly to save the entire world, and You paid dearly to save me. I'm sorry for the mistakes I've made in my life. I'm sorry for the times I've turned my back on You and not been the person You created me to be. Thank You for the precious gift of Your Son, the only way to eternal life. Please come into my heart, Jesus. I give You first place in my life. I receive Your precious gift and surrender everything to You. I surrender this cancer to You, Lord. You are all I need. You are the only one who can save me.

New Life

*This means that anyone who belongs to Christ has
become a new person. The old life is gone;
a new life has begun!*
2 CORINTHIANS 5:17

Lord, thank You that Your Spirit took up residence in my spirit when I first believed. I'm not the same anymore! I'm not just improved or rehabilitated. I'm completely transformed! My old life is gone, and I'm a brand-new person on the inside. I have a new life with a new Master. Thank You, Lord, for this new beginning I have in You. Please make my life reflect Your power, Your presence, and Your promises. Please help my life to be a reflection of You.

By Faith Alone

*This Good News tells us how God makes us right in his sight.
This is accomplished from start to finish by faith. As the Scriptures
say, "It is through faith that a righteous person has life."*
ROMANS 1:17

God, You had a simple plan to save me. Thank You that my faith alone makes me right in Your sight! Unlike all other religions, I don't have to do anything to earn my salvation. Help me to accept and believe that this cancer is not the result of my not doing enough to be a good person, or falling short of Your standard. My relationship is made right with You from start to finish, only by believing and trusting in You. Thank You that I am made righteous by faith alone. Thank You for coming to save me!

By Grace Alone

*God saved you by his grace when you believed. And you can't
take credit for this; it is a gift from God. Salvation is not
a reward for the good things we have done,
so none of us can boast about it.*
EPHESIANS 2:8–9

Lord, thank You for the gift You have freely given me by Your grace alone, regardless of what I have done or left undone. Please forgive me when I try to earn my way to You, compare myself to others, or believe that I am more deserving than someone else. Your saving grace is not a reward for my efforts, ability, intelligence, or good deeds. All I can do is accept Your gift and respond to Your unearned favor with gratitude, praise, and joy! I praise You, Lord! Your grace is truly amazing.

You Are Saved

*If you openly declare that Jesus is Lord and believe in your heart that
God raised him from the dead, you will be saved. For it is by believing
in your heart that you are made right with God, and it is
by openly declaring your faith that you are saved.*
ROMANS 10:9–10

Thank You, Father, that the gift of eternal life is as close as my lips and my heart. You made the way so simple, Lord. Forgive me when I try to make it complicated! To be honest, Lord, sometimes it's humbling to know that I can't do anything to save myself and that I am fully dependent on You for my every breath. Help me never to doubt that Your death and resurrection are truly enough to save me. Help me believe in my heart that when You look at me, You truly see the righteousness of God! I openly declare that You are my Lord! I declare by faith that I am saved!

No Other Name

"There is salvation in no one else! God has given no other name under heaven by which we must be saved."
ACTS 4:12

Lord, sometimes it feels narrow and exclusive to believe You are the only way to God and there is salvation in no one else. But in truth, Your way is more inclusive than any other way that claims to be true. Your way is wide enough for the whole world to enter, regardless of our past. Yes, Lord, no other religious leader was nailed to a cross and suffered and died for me, no other religious leader came to earth as God in the flesh, and no other religious leader rose victoriously from the dead and conquered evil once and for all. Thank You, Lord, for making a sure way when there was no other way. No other name under heaven can save me.

⌒

Child of God

But to all who believed him and accepted him, he gave the right to become children of God. They are reborn—not with a physical birth resulting from human passion or plan, but a birth that comes from God.
JOHN 1:12–13

Heavenly Father, through my physical birth, I became a member of my earthly family. But through my spiritual rebirth, You made me a member of Your eternal family. Thank You for the new life I have in You! Thank You for transforming me from the inside out. Just as I didn't have to earn my salvation, I can't rely on my own strength to be worthy of being Your child. I only have to trust that, day by day, You are rearranging my attitudes, motives, and desires to align with Yours. I am truly a new creation, a child of Yours! Lord, thank You for the fresh start I have in You every day!

CLEAN SLATE

*But if we confess our sins to him, he is faithful
and just to forgive us our sins and to cleanse us from all wickedness.*
1 JOHN 1:9

Thank You, God, that when I confess my wrongdoings You are faithful to wipe my slate clean! You died for every mistake I ever made and will ever make. Lord, in Your eyes, my sin is as far away as the east is from the west. Since You don't remember my mistakes anymore, neither should I! Lord, please take away any guilt and shame I still carry about my past. Thank You that nothing I can ever do will separate me from Your love. Please help me to focus on the person You created me to be, instead of the sin debt You have already paid for me. I praise You, Lord! My relationship with You is secure, now and forevermore.

~

GIVER OF LIFE

*And this is what God has testified: He has given us eternal life,
and this life is in his Son. Whoever has the Son has life;
whoever does not have God's Son does not have life.*
1 JOHN 5:11–13

Lord, my eternal relationship with You began from the moment I first believed. I don't need to work for it, and I don't need to hope it will come to pass someday. My life in You is a done deal. It is not based on my feelings, my struggles, or even this cancer. I have life only because I have You! In You, I live and move and have my very existence. Thank You for Your assurance that I am Your child and You will never leave or forsake me. Help me to comprehend what this new life in You actually means, through good times and bad, in health and in sickness. Thank You, Lord, the Giver of Life!

Safe in His Hand

"I give them eternal life, and they will never perish. No one can snatch them away from me, for my Father has given them to me, and he is more powerful than anyone else. No one can snatch them from the Father's hand."
John 10:28–29

Father, You protect me just as a shepherd protects his flock. The devil may try to steal, kill, and destroy on this earth, but You protect me from all his strategies and tricks. Despite his empty threats, the enemy and his cancer cannot touch my soul or take away my life with You. My life is no longer mortal and temporal; my life in You is eternal and forever. You conquered the enemy at Calvary and took away the sting of death. You died so I could live. Thank You that I am safe forever in Your hand.

Freedom from the Law

"Yet we know that a person is made right with God by faith in Jesus Christ, not by obeying the law. And we have believed in Christ Jesus, so that we might be made right with God because of our faith in Christ, not because we have obeyed the law. For no one will ever be made right with God by obeying the law."
Galatians 2:16

Lord, when I think of trying to follow the law, I am so thankful You made another way! Yes, the law gives me standards for how to behave and convicts me when I go astray. Best of all, it points me to You! But, Lord, I could never follow the law on my own power. Following all the rules or trying to be a good person can never heal me or make me whole. Forgive me when I forget and fall into the trap of trying to earn Your favor by doing all the right things. You know the motives of my heart, Lord. Nothing I can do on my own power can ever save me. Faith in You alone can save me. Only You, Lord. Help me to trust You. You are the best gift I will ever receive.

Chapter 6: His Message

The Fullness of the Good News

"God anointed Jesus of Nazareth with the Holy Spirit and with power. Then Jesus went around doing good and healing all who were oppressed by the devil, for God was with Him."
ACTS 10:38

My child, as you seek Me for healing, I want you to understand the fullness of My message of hope. When I was on earth, the Good News wasn't only what I said about salvation, but what I actually *did*. I combined preaching about forgiveness with healing the sick and expelling demons as a *demonstration* of the fullness of My Gospel message. No, I didn't just come to explain the way to eternal life. I came to proclaim the Good News to the poor, to proclaim freedom for the prisoners and recovery of sight for the blind, to set the oppressed free, and to proclaim that My favor has come (Luke 4:18–19)!

My message of hope didn't stop with Me. First, I gave My twelve disciples power and authority to cast out all demons and to heal all diseases in My name. I sent them out to tell everyone about the kingdom (Luke 9:1–2). Then I chose seventy-two other disciples and sent them out in pairs to heal the sick and share the Good News. They rejoiced because they were able to heal the sick and cast out demons when they used My name (Luke 10:1–3, 9, 17). Finally, I gave the same mission to everyone who believes in Me. I sent them into the world to preach the Good News to everyone everywhere. I promised that signs and wonders would follow them and they would be able to place their hands on the sick and heal them (Mark 16:15–18). Yes, beloved, *anyone* who believes in Me will do the same works I have done, and even greater works (John 14:12)!

After I ascended into heaven, I continued to show through My followers that healing and miracles were a central and vital part of My Church and My message to the world. When Peter prayed for boldness in preaching, He also asked for the power to do healing miracles through My name (Acts 4:29–30). My servant Paul fully presented the Good News by his message of hope and by the miraculous signs and wonders he worked among the people (Romans 15:18–19).

My child, My message hasn't changed! I want you to experience the fullness of salvation I won for you on the cross. I was beaten so you could be whole and you were healed by My stripes (Isaiah 53:4–5). Dear one, My healing grace touches your whole body, soul, and spirit. In the Bible, I use the Greek word *sozo* 110 times to capture the fullness of My Gospel message. It means "to save or make well or whole." For example, in Romans 10:9, I save [sozo] your spirit: "If you openly declare that Jesus is Lord and believe in your heart that God raised him from the dead, you will be saved [sozo]." In Matthew 9:22, I heal [sozo] your body: "'Daughter, be encouraged! Your faith has made you well [sozo].' And the woman was healed [sozo] at that moment." And in Luke 8:36, I deliver [sozo] your soul: "Then those who had seen what happened told the others how the demon-possessed man had been healed [sozo]."

Child, My message of hope offers salvation from eternal destruction, physical healing, and freedom from demonic strongholds. I came to sozo you: to save, heal, and deliver!

PRAY

To Be Whole

Now may the God of peace make you holy in every way,
and may your whole spirit and soul and body be kept blameless
until our Lord Jesus Christ comes again.
1 Thessalonians 5:23

Lord, thank You for the whole person You have created me to be. Starting with the first human being, You made my physical body out of dust and breathed life into it. You have given me a soul, a unique personality consisting of my mind, will, and emotions. Your spirit took up residence in my spirit when I first believed, giving me the ability to connect with You and understand Your spiritual truth. Thank You that Your Gospel message touches my whole being: body, soul, and spirit. Keep me blameless, Lord, through Your precious gift of salvation.

Good News

"The Spirit of the Lord is on me, because he has anointed me to proclaim
good news to the poor. He has sent me to proclaim freedom for
the prisoners and recovery of sight for the blind, to set the
oppressed free, to proclaim the year of the Lord's favor."
Luke 4:18–19 niv

Jesus, when You quoted Isaiah's prophecy in the synagogue at Nazareth, You made Your mission clear to the world. You told them this prophecy had come to pass before their very eyes. You were the anointed one they were waiting for, the one who would proclaim good news to the poor and freedom for the prisoners, recover sight for the blind, and set the oppressed free! Lord, thank You that Your mission was more than to announce the Good News of the kingdom, but to demonstrate Your message by Your actions!

Message of Hope

*Jesus traveled through all the towns and villages of that area,
teaching in the synagogues and announcing the Good News
about the Kingdom. And he healed every kind of disease and illness.*
MATTHEW 9:35

Lord, when You were here on earth, You did more than announce the promise of eternal life sometime in the future. You engaged with your people and met their needs of the day. You healed every kind of disease and illness. In fact, much of Your ministry included physical healing. I'm sorry for limiting Your message of hope to the precious gift of salvation. Thank You, Lord, that my eternity with You is assured. My long-awaited Messiah has come to save me! Lord, like those from the towns and villages who gathered around You to hear You preach the Good News of the kingdom, I need Your healing touch today. Lord, I need Your message of hope.

His Word Fulfilled

*That evening many demon-possessed people were brought to Jesus.
He cast out the evil spirits with a simple command, and he healed all
the sick. This fulfilled the word of the Lord through the prophet Isaiah,
who said, "He took our sicknesses and removed our diseases."*
MATTHEW 8:16–17

Father, the prophet Isaiah said You would come to take away sickness and remove diseases. And You did just that. With a single touch, You healed the sick. A single word caused demons to flee from Your presence! Lord, You have authority over all evil power and earthly disease. And You have power and authority over this cancer that threatens to destroy my future. Thank You for fulfilling Your word in my life. You are my only hope.

Saved

*"For the Son of Man came to seek
and save those who are lost."*
Luke 19:10

Lord, thank You for Your relentless pursuit when I was lost! You are the only one with the power to save (sozo) my spirit from eternal destruction. Thank You for Your message of hope that promises eternal life for all who believe, regardless of the past. I was lost, but now I'm found. By Your grace, You saved me, Lord!

Healed

*And Jesus said to him, "Go, for your faith has healed you."
Instantly the man could see, and he followed Jesus down the road.*
Mark 10:52

Thank You, God, that physical healing is part of Your redemptive grace and the Good News of Your kingdom. You are the only one with the power to heal (sozo) me and restore my body. Thank You that by faith there is healing for my body and I can be free of sickness and disease! Thank You for Your message of hope that touches this cancer in my body. By Your grace, You healed me, Lord!

Delivered

Then those who had seen what happened told the others
how the demon-possessed man had been healed.
Luke 8:36

Lord, thank You that deliverance from demonic strongholds is part of Your redemptive grace and the Good News of Your kingdom. You are the only One with the power to deliver (sozo) me from evil. Thank You that by faith there is healing for my soul and I can be free from the lies of the enemy! Thank You for Your message of hope that touches my mind, will, and emotions. By Your grace, You delivered me, Lord. I am free!

His Full Authority

"Is it easier to say 'Your sins are forgiven,' or 'Stand up and walk'?
So I will prove to you that the Son of Man has the authority
on earth to forgive sins." Then Jesus turned to the paralyzed man
and said, "Stand up, pick up your mat, and go home!"
And the man jumped up and went home!
Matthew 9:5–7

Jesus, when You were here, people had no problem accepting and believing You could heal the sick. Their problem was in believing that You could forgive their sins and save them from eternal destruction. Ironically, today we have no problem accepting You as our only way to heaven, but we often struggle with believing You still heal the sick. Lord, You showed people You had both the power to forgive and the power to heal! Whether You said "your sins are forgiven" or "stand up and walk," the results would be the same. You saved, healed, and delivered the lost, the sick, and the oppressed. Thank You that Your message of hope accomplished it all!

Commissioning the Twelve

"Go and announce to them that the Kingdom of Heaven is near.
Heal the sick, raise the dead, cure those with leprosy,
and cast out demons. Give as freely as you have received!"
Matthew 10:7–8

Lord, You announced the coming of Your kingdom by preaching, healing, and casting out demons. You demonstrated there was more to salvation than eternal life. When You sent out Your twelve disciples on the same mission, You gave them the same power and authority. They shared the Good News, but their message wasn't complete without the power and authority to heal the sick, raise the dead, cure the lepers, and cast out demons! Thank You, Lord, for the fullness of Your Gospel message. In this battle for wellness, help me to receive the full reward for Your suffering.

Commissioning the Seventy-Two

"Heal the sick, and tell them, 'The Kingdom of God is near you now. . . .'
Then he said to the disciples, 'Anyone who accepts your message is
also accepting me. And anyone who rejects you is rejecting me.
And anyone who rejects me is rejecting God, who sent me.'"
Luke 10:9, 16

Jesus, You gave the seventy-two the same authority to share Your message of hope. You made it clear that Your message included healing the sick, and if they rejected Your message, they were rejecting You. Empowered by the Spirit, they had the same results as You! They preached the Good News, healed the sick, and cast out demons in Your name. Lord, when You brought the kingdom to earth, You started a movement that is still alive today. Thank You for showing us we can walk in Your footsteps. Empowered by Your Spirit, nothing is impossible.

The Great Commission

And then he told them, "Go into all the world and preach the Good News to everyone. Anyone who believes and is baptized will be saved. But anyone who refuses to believe will be condemned. These miraculous signs will accompany those who believe: They will cast out demons in my name, and they will speak in new languages. They will be able to handle snakes with safety, and if they drink anything poisonous, it won't hurt them. They will be able to place their hands on the sick, and they will be healed."
MARK 16:15–18

Your great commission clearly shows You sent us into the world, Lord, just as You sent the twelve and the seventy-two. You spread your message of hope through Your disciples, and You commissioned Your early Church and all of us to do the same today: to save, heal, and deliver people in Your name. Lord, I look forward to eternal life, and I long for the day You will return to earth to destroy evil once and for all. While I anticipate my glorious future, forgive me for forgetting about the power You have given me today! Lord, please lead me to people who walk in the fullness of Your authority, people who cast out demons and place their hands on the sick and see them be healed. Help me to both experience and share the fullness of the Good News!

Greater Works

*"I tell you the truth, anyone who believes in me will do
the same works I have done, and even greater works,
because I am going to be with the Father."*
John 14:12

Lord, when I ponder the miraculous signs and wonders You did on earth, I can't even imagine Your believers doing greater works! But Lord, since this is Your plan and this is Your promise, I pray it will come to pass! I pray that healing of cancer and all sickness and disease will be commonplace in churches, clinics, and hospitals around the country as people spread Your message of hope. Let revival spread across my city, my state, the nation, and the entire world! Lord, may signs, wonders, and miracles be widespread as people bow down to Your holy and precious name! May there be greater works beyond anything I can ask for or imagine.

Great Boldness

*"And now, O Lord, hear their threats, and give us, your servants,
great boldness in preaching your word. Stretch out your hand with
healing power; may miraculous signs and wonders be done
through the name of your holy servant Jesus." After this prayer,
the meeting place shook, and they were all filled with the Holy
Spirit. Then they preached the word of God with boldness.*
Acts 4:29–31

In the New Testament, You showed us clearly how Your Church should be. The early believers not only prayed for great boldness in preaching, but they asked You for healing power to do miraculous signs and wonders in Your name! You answered their prayer, Lord! When the crowds came to hear them preach, they brought their sick and all who were oppressed by evil spirits. *All* were healed, every single one! Lord, please give me the boldness to press on through my fears and doubts. Help me to expect You to act according to Your promises!

Fullness of the Gospel

Yet I dare not boast about anything except what Christ has done through me, bringing the Gentiles to God by my message and by the way I worked among them. They were convinced by the power of miraculous signs and wonders and by the power of God's Spirit. In this way, I have fully presented the Good News of Christ from Jerusalem all the way to Illyricum.
Romans 15:18–19

Lord, You demonstrated through Your apostle Paul what it truly means to fully present the Good News. He brought the Gentiles Your message of hope by preaching and working among them, in the same way You did while you were here on earth. And the people were convinced by the power of miraculous signs and wonders and by the power of Your Spirit. Lord, I receive the fullness of Your Gospel message: salvation from eternal destruction, healing for my body, and freedom from demonic strongholds.

Chapter 7: His Compassion

The Good Shepherd

When he saw the crowds, he had compassion on them because they were confused and helpless, like sheep without a shepherd.
MATTHEW 9:36

They murdered him. My cousin John, the one sent to pave the way for My ministry, beheaded by King Herod as a reward for a young girl's pleasing dance performance. My heart ached and tears stung My eyes at the thought of such a senseless and brutal act. I tried to slip away by boat to a remote area to be alone. I needed to pray and grieve, to process what had just happened. But instead of finding solitude when I stepped off the boat, I found a vast crowd of people waiting for Me. There were cripples, lepers, the blind and deaf, and hordes of sick people all shouting at once, "Teacher, touch me! Make me well again!" They all pushed and shoved toward Me, clamoring for My attention. But I couldn't bear to send them away. Compassion rose from deep within Me. I set My own grief aside, and I healed them all (Matthew 14:1–14).

My child, do you understand? I didn't heal all those who came to Me just to prove My power came from heaven. No, I saved and healed them because I have deep compassion for the sick and oppressed. As I looked over this crowd, My heart broke for them. They were like sheep without a shepherd. Their needs were so great, and they didn't know where to go for help. Like lost sheep, they wandered aimlessly through life, sick and broken, alone and hopeless, desperate for a Shepherd who would come to lead and guide them. They desperately needed My love, protection, comfort, and healing.

Throughout the ages, I have showered My unfailing love and compassion on My creation (Psalm 25:6). It was compassion that led Me to restore Israel even though My people repeatedly failed to follow My warnings to turn from their sin (Zechariah 10:6). It was compassion that overflowed in My heart when I raised the only son of a widow from the dead (Luke 7:13–15). Compassion moved Me to pity a begging man and heal him from leprosy (Mark 1:41). Compassion compelled Me to weep when My dear friend Lazarus died and his sisters grieved (John 11:35).

Beloved, as you face this cancer, I have the same compassion for you. I know every tear you cry in your pillow at night (Psalm 6:6–10). I keep track of your sorrows and collect every tear (Psalm 56:8). I know the fears you face each day (Psalm 27:1–3), and I hear your every cry for help (Psalm 57:2–3). I know your despair when I seem far away (Psalm 22:10–13), even though I have never once left your side (Psalm 139:7). Yes, I am fighting for you (Psalm 18:4–19). My compassion compels Me to do nothing less.

My child, you have a Savior who can sympathize with your weaknesses (Hebrews 4:15). I truly understand the depths of your pain. I Myself have endured much. I cried your tears, suffered your wounds, and felt every human emotion you will ever feel. I was mocked, spat on, whipped, beaten beyond recognition, and died a criminal's death. It wasn't necessary for them to pierce My hands and feet and nail Me to the cross. My compassion for you would have held Me there.

PRAY

The Father's Heart

*The LORD is like a father to his children, tender and compassionate
to those who fear him. For he knows how weak we are;
he remembers we are only dust.*
Psalm 103:13–14

Like an earthly father, You know I am as fragile and helpless as a
small child. But You, Lord, are a perfect Father, and Your compassion
is eternal. Forgive me for believing You are a distant, cold, or judging
Father who withholds Your love and compassion when I don't measure up to Your expectations. Lord, thank You for understanding my
humanness and for remembering my weakness as I struggle to walk
in faith. In Your compassion, help me to trust You.

Strength for Battle

*But you, O Lord, are a God of compassion and mercy, slow to get
angry and filled with unfailing love and faithfulness. Look down and
have mercy on me. Give your strength to your servant;
save me, the son of your servant.*
Psalm 86:15–16

Lord, this cancer attacked my body when I was weakest. Every day,
it continues to rise up against me, threatening to steal my hopes
and dreams. But You, Lord, are a God of compassion and mercy,
filled with unfailing love and faithfulness. Please Lord, show me
Your mercy! I am Your humble servant. Give me Your strength to
fight this enemy. Help me and comfort me. Save me, Lord! Put this
cancer to shame.

Unfailing Compassion

Remember, O Lord, your compassion and unfailing love,
which you have shown from long ages past.
Psalm 25:6

Father, You had compassion from the very beginning when Your first children disobeyed and were expelled from the garden. You have had compassion through the ages, even though Your people have repeatedly failed to follow Your commands and turn from their sin. It was compassion that drove You to the cross to redeem a broken, sinful world. Lord, I need Your compassion right now. I want to believe that Your heart longs to help me, that You feel deep sorrow for my pain and suffering in the midst of the battle that rages within me. Remember Your compassion, Lord. Help me to trust You.

Compassion to Restore

"I will strengthen Judah and save Israel; I will restore them
because of my compassion. It will be as though I had never rejected
them, for I am the Lord their God, who will hear their cries."
Zechariah 10:6

It is Your compassion that compels You to restore my brokenness, Lord. You are the God who restores all things. You restore broken kingdoms, broken relationships, broken bodies, and broken hearts. Just as You forgave Judah and Israel, forgive me for the times I have turned my back on You to follow my own agenda and the trappings of the world. Thank You for hearing my cries for help. Thank You for never remembering my failures and shortcomings. Lord, thank You for Your compassion to restore.

Compassion for the Suffering

Sing for joy, O heavens! Rejoice, O earth! Burst into song, O mountains!
For the LORD has comforted his people and will have
compassion on them in their suffering.
ISAIAH 49:13

God, thank You that You have never forgotten me. It is no more possible for You to forget me than for a loving mother to forget her very own child. Even when I have drifted far away from You and I can't feel Your presence, You are with me, ready to pour out Your love and compassion and ready to comfort me in my suffering. You know the depths of my pain, Lord. You know how this diagnosis torments me in so many ways. Nothing escapes You. I sing for joy, Lord. I rejoice in the comfort only You can offer.

Compassion for Those Who Wait

So the LORD must wait for you to come to him so he can show
you his love and compassion. For the LORD is a faithful
God. Blessed are those who wait for his help.
ISAIAH 30:18

Lord, only You can carry me through this journey that never ends. I come to You, Lord. Forgive me if I've been tempted to push You away. I invite You into the middle of this trial so You can show me Your love and compassion. You are so faithful, Lord! Thank You for being with me, loving me, teaching me, guiding me, and comforting me. I wait for Your help, Lord. Please give me peace as I wait for Your promises to fully manifest.

Compassion for Those in Pain

Have compassion on me, LORD, for I am weak.
Heal me, LORD, for my bones are in agony.
PSALM 6:2

You know how weak I am, Father. My body aches, my pain is excruciating, and my bones are in agony. How long must I wait for You to heal and restore me? Yet, You are holy. Have compassion on me, Lord. Comfort me in this affliction! You are the God who heals all my diseases. Please take this pain away. Heal me, Lord! Make me whole again.

Compassion for the Depressed

I waited patiently for the LORD to help me, and he turned to me
and heard my cry. He lifted me out of the pit of despair,
out of the mud and the mire. He set my feet on solid
ground and steadied me as I walked along.
PSALM 40:1–2

Lord, how long must I wait? My heart is heavy and darkness surrounds me. I feel my feet sinking deeper and deeper into the pit of despair. Hear my cry, Lord! Pull me out of the mud and the mire! Set my feet on solid ground and steady me as I walk through this valley of cancer. I need You, Lord. I can't do this alone. You are the Light in my darkness. You are my only hope in the battle against hopelessness. You are all I need.

COMPASSION TO SAVE

Death wrapped its ropes around me; the terrors of the grave overtook me. I saw only trouble and sorrow. Then I called on the name of the LORD: "Please, LORD, save me!" How kind the LORD is! How good he is! So merciful, this God of ours!
PSALM 116:3–5

The terrors of the grave threaten to overtake me, and the fear of death torments me. Lord, I call on Your name. Bend down and listen to my cries! Please, Lord, save me! Deliver me from this trouble and sorrow! Thank You for Your kindness and mercy. Yes, Lord, I will pray for as long as I have breath because I know You will hear and answer my prayers. You are a God of compassion, a God who saves.

COMPASSION TO ANSWER

For he will rescue you from every trap and protect you from deadly disease. . . . The LORD says, "I will rescue those who love me. I will protect those who trust in my name. When they call on me, I will answer; I will be with them in trouble. I will rescue and honor them."
PSALM 91:3, 14–15

Lord, thank You for Your promise to rescue and protect me from this deadly disease, cancer. Lord, I love You. I trust in Your name! Please be with me through this trouble. Be with me through every doctor appointment, every blood test, every scan, and every treatment. Lord, protect me from the side effects as potent drugs flow through my body threatening to kill the good cells along with the bad. Rescue me, Lord! Thank You for answering my call for help.

Compassion for the Repentant

"So he returned home to his father. And while he was still a long way off, his father saw him coming. Filled with love and compassion, he ran to his son, embraced him, and kissed him."
Luke 15:20

In my weakness, heavenly Father, I can drift out of fellowship with You just as the prodigal son left his father for a life of worldly pleasures. Sometimes this journey through cancer consumes me. Every day I have opportunities to take my eyes off You, distracted by my circumstances and worldly thinking. But You are merciful and compassionate, eager to welcome me home with an embrace and a kiss. Forgive me, Lord, when I have put my trust in anything or anyone other than You for my healing and restoration. Forgive me when I have insisted on my own agenda. Thank You that You are always with me and You never leave me or forsake me.

Compassion for the Sick

Moved with compassion, Jesus reached out and touched him. "I am willing," he said. "Be healed!"
Mark 1:41

Lord, You had great compassion for this man with leprosy in a culture that shunned him and regarded him as unclean. I can only imagine how hungry he was for human touch after being separated from his family for so long. But You, Lord, reached out in love and touched him. You saw a child You created in Your image suffering from a devastating sickness, and You healed him and made him whole. You can do the same for me, Lord. Reach out and touch me, Lord. Let me hear You speak the words, "be healed."

Compassion for Those Who Mourn

When the Lord saw her, his heart overflowed with compassion.
"Don't cry!" he said. Then he walked over to the coffin and touched it,
and the bearers stopped. "Young man," he said, "I tell you,
get up." Then the dead boy sat up and began to talk!
And Jesus gave him back to his mother.
Luke 7:13–15

This woman's son died, leaving her helpless, alone, and destined for a life of begging. When You saw her, Jesus, grieving for her lost son and her hopeless future, Your heart overflowed with compassion. You were the only hope for her impossible circumstances, so You reached out and did the impossible. You turned her tragedy into triumph. Please, Lord, let Your compassion overflow into my impossible circumstances. Just as You gave this son back to his mother, please give me back my life.

Compassion for Those Who Weep

Then Jesus wept.
John 11:35

Lord, although You were fully God while You walked on this earth, You were also fully human. You were whipped, beaten, bloodied, and misunderstood. You suffered unimaginable pain and persecution and a brutal death at the hands of Your enemies, while even Your own disciples deserted You. Lord, forgive me when I forget that You are no stranger to my pain. Just as You wept for Mary and Martha as they grieved the death of their brother Lazarus, You also weep for me. You feel my pain, and You understand my sorrow. I am humbled, Lord. Thank You for the compassion that drove You to the cross, that same compassion that comforts and heals me.

Chapter 8: His Will

I Want You Well

*A man with leprosy came and knelt in front of Jesus,
begging to be healed. "If you are willing, you can heal me
and make me clean," he said. Moved with compassion,
Jesus reached out and touched him. "I am willing," he said. "Be healed!"*

MARK 1:40–41

"Lord, if it be Your will. . ." My child, so often I hear you say this when you cry out to Me for healing. I know you do it out of your reverence for Me and My sovereignty. I love it when your heart's desire is to be in alignment with My plan. But child, do you ever pray this way to give yourself an out, rather than as an act of full surrender to Me? Instead of standing in faith that you will receive what you ask for, are you preparing yourself in advance for Me to say no? It is logical to conclude that your prayer is outside of My will if you don't receive what you hope for or expect. But is it possible, My child, that you didn't pray according *to* My will?

When you pray for physical healing, you can be assured of My will! A healthy body is a reflection of My goodness and My abundant love for you. I grieve over all human brokenness, and I want you to be completely whole (1 Thessalonians 5:23–24). My child, sickness and death were never part of My original plan. I created, called My creation good, and I gave you dominion over the earth (Genesis 1:31). Then sickness entered the world along with sin, and My beautiful creation fell into decay (Genesis 3:7; Romans 5:12). But I came to take back what the enemy stole from you and restore all things (Colossians 1:20). I came to destroy the works of the devil (1 John 3:8) and heal your diseases by the stripes on My back (Isaiah 53:5).

Beloved, when you ask Me for healing only if it is My will, are you not really praying, "Lord, if it's not Your will to heal me, then let this cancer take me?" No, My child, this is not My nature. When I was here on earth, no one who came to Me ever walked away without their healing, and I never turned a person's request for healing down. There are many times when I healed *all* who came (Acts 10:38; Matthew 8:16; 12:15; 4:24; Luke 6:19). I never prayed "if it be Your will" prayers for healing, and neither did My disciples. I came to save, heal, and deliver and left My disciples and all believers with the mandate to "place their hands on the sick, and they will be healed" (Mark 16:18). We directed our prayers at the problem and prayed with authority, speaking commands like, "Pick up your mat, and walk" (John 5:8) or "Be healed" (Luke 5:13).

My child, let Me gently ask you this question: If it's not My will for you to be well, why are you seeking medical help for this cancer? If you believe it's possible for Me to want you sick, and you are seeking healing through medical care, wouldn't you be acting against My will? No, I want to heal because it's My nature to heal. My love and compassion compels Me to heal. I planned for you to live a long, full, and satisfying life (Psalm 91:16; John 10:10). I promised to care for you throughout your lifetime—until your hair is white with age (Isaiah 46:4)! Dear one, it delights Me that you want My will for your life. But I need you to agree with Me on this: I want you well.

PRAY

THE LORD WHO HEALS

He said, "If you will listen carefully to the voice of the LORD your God
and do what is right in his sight, obeying his commands and keeping
all his decrees, then I will not make you suffer any of the diseases
I sent on the Egyptians; for I am the LORD who heals you."
EXODUS 15:26

Lord, You are the God who heals me! Thank You for the natural laws
You have put into place to keep me safe and well. Thank You for my
immune system and other body systems You have created within me
to heal and restore. Lord, in Your holy and precious name, I call on
my immune system now to fight this cancer! Strengthen me, Lord!
The doctors will fight with human wisdom, but You are the Lord
who heals me!

BY HIS STRIPES

He personally carried our sins in his body on the cross
so that we can be dead to sin and live for what
is right. By his wounds you are healed.
1 PETER 2:24

You are the Lamb of God, the perfect sacrifice for the sin of the
world. Isaiah prophesied that You would come to save me, and You
did! You personally carried my sins and sickness in Your body on the
cross. You are the Suffering Servant who came to set me free! I can't
find human words to thank You, Lord. There are no words. Yet, You
would have done it just for me. Yes, by Your wounds, I am healed. It
is finished.

Healing in His Wings

*"But for you who fear my name, the Sun of Righteousness will rise
with healing in his wings. And you will go free, leaping with joy
like calves let out to pasture. On the day when I act,
you will tread upon the wicked as if they were dust under
your feet," says the LORD of Heaven's Armies.*
MALACHI 4:2–3

Creator of all things, You placed the sun and the moon and the stars in the sky! The warmth of Your sunlight radiates over and through my body as You wrap Your loving arms around me, holding me safe and secure. You are the Light in my darkness, Lord. You are my only certainty in a world of uncertainty. You are my only hope in a world that threatens to steal my hope. Tread on this cancer, Lord. Trample it under Your feet until it becomes like dust. Then I will rise with healing in my wings. Release me from this cancer that holds me captive and set me free! I leap for joy, Lord. My future is in You alone.

Promise of Deliverance

*"I will give you back your health
and heal your wounds," says the LORD.*
JEREMIAH 30:17

Lord, You are so good to Your people! Even when they were held captive in Babylon as a result of their disobedience, You promised to deliver them and avenge the injustice they suffered at the hands of their enemies. Please, Lord, do the same for me. Free me from my Babylon. Release me from this cancer. Restore what the enemy has stolen from me. Forgive me when I put all my trust in worldly cures and treatments when You are the only one who can deliver me. Thank You for giving me back my health.

The Sick Restored

Oh, the joys of those who are kind to the poor! The LORD rescues
them when they are in trouble. The LORD protects them
and keeps them alive. He gives them prosperity in the land
and rescues them from their enemies. The LORD nurses
them when they are sick and restores them to health.
PSALM 41:1–3

You are so kind to me, Father! I am in trouble, but You promise to rescue me! My life is in danger, but You promise to protect me and keep me alive! Lord, when my earthly doctors and nurses care for me, it is Your loving touch I feel through their hands. You are the one who nurses me when I am sick and restores me to health. Thank You, Lord. Thank You for Your compassion and tender mercies. Rescue me, Lord! Rescue me from this cancer!

Good Things

Let all that I am praise the LORD; may I never forget the good things
he does for me. He forgives all my sins and heals all my diseases.
PSALM 103:2–3

King David praised You, God, for Your glorious deeds, and so do I! No matter how dire my circumstances become, help me to always count my blessings. You are the God who forgives all my sins and heals all my diseases. Lord, thank You for the good health I have enjoyed over the years. Thank You for my family, my friends, my talents and gifts, my home, and all the ways You provide for me. Thank You for life itself. Most of all, thank You for the cross and the gift of Your eternal presence in my life. I have so many reasons to praise You, Lord, I can't even begin to list them all! Help me never to forget the good things You do for me.

Healed by His Word

"Lord, help!" they cried in their trouble, and he saved them
from their distress. He sent out his word and healed
them, snatching them from the door of death.
Psalm 107:19–20

You saved the wanderer, the prisoner, the storm-tossed, and the distressed. You merely spoke, sending out Your word, and people were healed, snatched from the door of death. I am in distress, Lord, and You are the only one who can save me. I cry to You in my trouble, "Lord, help!" Thank You for Your loving kindness and Your heart to heal me. Snatch me now, Lord. Rescue me from this cancer. I want to be a witness to Your faithfulness and healing power. To You be the glory forevermore.

His Word Brings Life

My child, pay attention to what I say. Listen carefully to my words.
Don't lose sight of them. Let them penetrate deep into your heart,
for they bring life to those who find them,
and healing to their whole body.
Proverbs 4:20–22

Lord, Your Word is the true medicine that heals. It is the source of my hope and my every breath. Help me to listen carefully and never lose sight of Your Word through the distractions of the world. Lord, I want Your Word to penetrate the depths of my heart. I want to live by Your Word and receive all the benefits of knowing You. Thank You that Your Word brings life and healing to my whole body.

Healing for Your Body

Don't be impressed with your own wisdom. Instead, fear the LORD
and turn away from evil. Then you will have healing
for your body and strength for your bones.
PROVERBS 3:7–8

Father, You are present in the eye of my storm, always guiding and directing my path. There is so much information and so many decisions! It overwhelms me, Lord, especially when the world's wisdom and my own understanding are at odds with Yours. Lord, help me to bring every decision to You and follow Your lead. Help me not to be wise in my own eyes, but to trust You completely. Then I will have healing for my body and strength for my bones.

$\sim$

Anointed to Heal

And you know that God anointed Jesus of Nazareth with the Holy
Spirit and with power. Then Jesus went around doing good and healing
all who were oppressed by the devil, for God was with him.
ACTS 10:38

Jesus, You showed Your heart and compassion for doing good and healing the sick when You walked this earth as a man. God anointed You with the Holy Spirit and the power to heal all who were oppressed by the enemy. Lord, You said Your followers would do even greater things! Thank You for giving Your followers the power and authority to share the Good News and heal the sick in Your name.

He Healed Them All

Jesus traveled throughout the region of Galilee, teaching in the synagogues and announcing the Good News about the Kingdom. And he healed every kind of disease and illness. News about him spread as far as Syria, and people soon began bringing to him all who were sick. And whatever their sickness or disease, or if they were demon possessed or epileptic or paralyzed—he healed them all.
MATTHEW 4:23–24

Lord, when You were here on earth, You didn't just heal *some* people and *some* sickness and diseases. You healed every single person who came to You with every kind of disease and illness. Lord, the coming of Your kingdom made healing possible then as well as today. Forgive me for doubting Your will to heal. Thank You that Your heart's desire for me is to be healed and whole.

⌒

All Healed

As a result of the apostles' work, sick people were brought out into the streets on beds and mats so that Peter's shadow might fall across some of them as he went by. Crowds came from the villages around Jerusalem, bringing their sick and those possessed by evil spirits, and they were all healed.
ACTS 5:15–16

Through Your apostles You continued to show Your will to heal the sick and cast out demons. Even those touched by Peter's shadow were healed by the power of Your Spirit! You are amazing, Lord. Indeed, You did greater works through Your followers. You demonstrated Your desire to heal in the early church, and I know it's possible for You to heal me today. I come to You, Lord. Draw me close. Let Your Spirit fall on me.

The Gift of Healing

The same Spirit gives great faith to another,
and to someone else the one Spirit gives the gift of healing.
1 Corinthians 12:9

Lord, thank You for the gifts of the Spirit that help build Your Church and advance Your kingdom here on earth. Thank You for coming to reconcile the world to Yourself and to destroy the works of the enemy! Thank You for inviting all who are willing to collaborate with You until Your finished work on the cross is completed here on earth. Thank You for the gift of healing. Please lead me to people who believe in Your heart's desire to heal and restore. May Your Spirit empower those who pray for healing in Your name.

He Never Changes

Jesus Christ is the same yesterday, today, and forever.
Hebrews 13:8

Lord God, You never change! By the power of Your Spirit, You healed in the Old Testament. You healed the sick when You walked on earth; Your disciples healed the sick in the early church, and by the same Spirit, You heal the sick today! Lord, I believe it is Your heart's desire to heal and restore. I believe You want me well. Thank You for being my solid rock in a world made of shifting sand. You are an unchanging God in a changing world!

Chapter 9: His Guidance

Perfect Alignment

When the Spirit of truth comes, he will guide you into all truth.
He will not speak on his own but will tell you what
he has heard. He will tell you about the future.
JOHN 16:13

My child, I made you in My image. You are wonderfully complex, a product of My marvelous workmanship (Psalm 139:14)! I created you in three interconnected parts—your body, your soul, and your spirit. Your body is made up of organs and cells and many intricate body systems, with an outward appearance that is uniquely yours. I gave you a soul, your unique personality consisting of your mind, will, and emotions. Your mind is where you think, reason, make plans, hold your attitudes and beliefs, and experience feelings. I gave you a self-directed will to allow you to make free choices.

Beloved, I created you to communicate and have eternal fellowship with Me through your spirit. Before I left this earth, I promised to send a counselor, the Holy Spirit, to guide you in all truth. My Spirit would reveal My standard for right living because I would no longer be physically present (John 16:8–13). Through My Spirit, I promised I would live in you and never leave you, comfort you, help you discern right from wrong, and teach you how to live according to My plan for your life (John 14:16–18, 26). When I became your Savior, My Spirit took up residence in your spirit, and you became a new person no longer obligated to follow your sinful nature (Romans 8:16).

I planned for your body, soul, and spirit to be divinely aligned and interconnected. When you are in perfect alignment, My Spirit rules over your soul and your soul rules over your body. When you allow My Spirit to lead, you can begin to know My thoughts and communicate with Me in prayer. You can trust I have given you a sound mind to make decisions (2 Timothy 1:7). When I give counsel through My medical realm, you can act with the best revelation you have and trust that doors will close or persistent uneasiness will trouble your spirit if you are moving outside of My plan.

Dear one, you must choose daily to submit to the Spirit and let Me guide and lead you. You can so easily fall out of alignment when your soul takes over and you allow your old nature to rule. My servant Paul spoke truth when he said, "Letting your sinful nature control your mind leads to death. But letting the Spirit control your mind leads to life and peace" (Romans 8:6). Living by the soul's thoughts, desires, and emotions can pull you back into the world and cut you off from My power. Unchecked emotions like worry, fear, and anxiety can take a toll on your body. Living by the Spirit instead of the soul allows you to hear My voice and receive My guidance and protection.

My child, let go of frustration and your soulish need to control your life. Trust Me for tomorrow. My plans are better than yours, and My timing is perfect. Feed your spirit each day with the promises of My Word. Allow new thought patterns to emerge that align with My truth instead of the thought patterns of the world. Cast your cares on Me and let My Spirit guide and lead you. Child, let me heal you from the inside out.

PRAY

Divine Alignment

*Dear friend, I hope all is well with you and that you are
as healthy in body as you are strong in spirit.*
3 John 1:2

Lord, thank You for making me to be so wonderfully complex! You created my body, soul, and spirit to function perfectly. You made my mind, will, and emotions to interact in perfect harmony with my body through my nervous system, immune system, and other body systems. Lord, my heart's desire is to walk in physical, emotional, and spiritual health. I want to live under Your authority and protection instead of my own thoughts, desires, and emotions. Lord, help me stay in alignment. Help me be as healthy in my body as I am strong in my spirit! Body, submit to my soul! Soul, submit to my spirit! Lord, I surrender to Your Spirit within me.

Thoughts of Heaven

Think about the things of heaven, not the things of earth.
Colossians 3:2

It's hard to keep my thoughts on heaven when this cancer battle consumes every day of my life. Forgive me for falling out of alignment when I allow worldly cares and concerns to dominate my thoughts instead of Your spirit within me. Help me to think on the lasting, eternal things of heaven instead of the concerns that are here today and gone tomorrow. Lord, help me to take Your view of this cancer. Break down the walls that keep me from surrendering my thoughts to You in the midst of this crisis. I cast my cares on You, Lord! I want to live under Your rule and reign, not my own! Help me to think about things of heaven.

A Renewed Mind

*Don't copy the behavior and customs of this world, but let God transform
you into a new person by changing the way you think. Then you will
learn to know God's will for you, which is good and pleasing and perfect.*
ROMANS 12:2

Father, forgive me when I forget You want the very best for me and
Your will is perfect. Help me to replace worry, stress, doubt, and
other unhealthy thoughts, emotions, and habits with the truth of
Your Word. Please give me new thought patterns that align with
Your truth instead of the enemy's lies and the customs of the world.
Every day, help me to live in obedience to Your Spirit instead of my
soul so I can hear Your voice, receive your protection, and begin to
be healed from the inside out. Lord, change my thinking! Renew my
mind so I can be truly transformed.

⁓

Divine Plans

*"My thoughts are nothing like your thoughts," says the LORD.
"And my ways are far beyond anything you could imagine. For just as
the heavens are higher than the earth, so my ways are higher than
your ways and my thoughts higher than your thoughts."*
ISAIAH 55:8–9

Your ways are higher than mine, far beyond anything I can imagine. When I submit to Your ways, I can always trust You to move
on my behalf. Thank You that Your timing is perfect and Your
knowledge and wisdom are far greater than mine, even greater
than my doctors' and caregivers'. Lord, forgive me when I push
You out of the driver's seat and take over the wheel! I'm sorry
when I try to make my plans without consulting You first. Give
me wisdom to make good plans and decisions, but help me to
hold on loosely. Pull me back into alignment, Lord, so my plans
and desires are Yours! Your plans and purposes are perfect, Lord.

Divine Guidance

So I say, let the Holy Spirit guide your lives. Then you won't be doing what your sinful nature craves. The sinful nature wants to do evil, which is just the opposite of what the Spirit wants. And the Spirit gives us desires that are the opposite of what the sinful nature desires. These two forces are constantly fighting each other, so you are not free to carry out your good intentions. But when you are directed by the Spirit, you are not under obligation to the law of Moses.
Galatians 5:16–18

Lord, by Your Spirit's leading, my heart's desire is for a life that produces love, joy, peace, patience, kindness, goodness, faithfulness, gentleness, and self-control. Lord, when I rely on my own wisdom, I risk making the wrong choices. If I try to follow You on my own power, I will fall short and disappoint myself. Only Your Spirit can give me the desire to hear Your voice, the willingness to obey Your Word, and the ability to discern the difference between Your promptings and my own thoughts, feelings, and desires. Guide me, Lord! I submit to Your Spirit! Help me live each day and make every decision under Your direction and control.

Divine Leading

Since we are living by the Spirit, let us follow the Spirit's leading in every part of our lives.
Galatians 5:25

Your Spirit leads every part of my life, Lord! Forgive me when I only surrender part of myself to Your leadership but hold other aspects of my life back from Your divine control. I surrender all of me, Lord! I submit my spiritual life to You, and I give You leadership over my job, my family, my social life, my thoughts, emotions, and intellect. Lord, I especially give You control over my health and my medical care. I give You complete control over this cancer, Lord. Your Spirit is my very life source, the power behind my every breath and every heartbeat. Lead me, Lord, and I will follow.

Divine Wisdom

*When we tell you these things, we do not use words that
come from human wisdom. Instead, we speak words given to us
by the Spirit, using the Spirit's words to explain spiritual truths.*
1 Corinthians 2:13

Thank You, Lord, for the gift of my spirit, the eternal part of me that communicates with You and understands Your truth. I can barely grasp that the God of heaven's armies, the same God who created the universe, actually lives in me and communicates directly to the spirit within me! Through Your Spirit and under Your authority and wisdom, the apostle Paul and others recorded Your very thoughts and words in the scriptures. Thank You, Lord, that in the same way, Your Spirit dwells within my spirit, and the very wisdom of heaven directs my path!

Divine Thoughts

*"Who can know the Lord's thoughts? Who knows enough
to teach him?" But we understand these things,
for we have the mind of Christ.*
1 Corinthians 2:16

Lord, how can I possibly know Your thoughts? Yet, Your Word says I can understand these things because I have the mind of Christ. Lord, help me continually surrender to the guidance of Your Spirit dwelling inside of me so I can begin to understand. Help me to spend time in Your presence and in Your Word so I can begin to know Your thoughts and Your plans. Lord, nothing makes sense to me right now, and I desperately want to understand. But I want You more.

Divine Comfort

For all who are led by the Spirit of God are children of God.
Romans 8:14

Father, thank You for reminding me that I am Your very own child. Just as a loving earthly mother guides, soothes, and nurtures her sick or injured child, Your Spirit cares for me. Lord, Your inward presence helps me focus on my identity as God's child and how much You love me. Help me remember that I am not a cancer patient or a cancer victim. My identity is in You alone. I am a child of the living God, and Your Spirit is my witness. Lead me, Lord. Lead me safely through the valley to the other side of this cancer.

Divine Advocacy

And the Holy Spirit helps us in our weakness. For example,
we don't know what God wants us to pray for. But the Holy Spirit
prays for us with groanings that cannot be expressed in words.
And the Father who knows all hearts knows what the Spirit is
saying, for the Spirit pleads for us believers
in harmony with God's own will.
Romans 8:26–27

There are days through this journey when I just can't muster up the strength or faith to pray. But even then, You promise to help me in my weakness. When I don't know what or how to pray, Your Spirit prays for me with groanings that cannot be expressed in words! I take great comfort in knowing You are pleading for me in harmony with God's own will! Lord, thank You! Thank You for knowing the deepest pleas of my heart. I trust You hear and will do what is best for me.

Divine Knowledge

But when the Father sends the Advocate as my representative—
that is, the Holy Spirit—he will teach you everything and
will remind you of everything I have told you.
John 14:26

Lord, You promised Your disciples that the Holy Spirit would help them remember what You taught them. They were eyewitnesses to Your life and teaching, so I can trust the Gospels are an accurate record of what You said and did. When I rest in Your presence and read Your Word, I can trust Your Spirit will remove the veil from my eyes and plant the same knowledge in my mind! Thank You for showing me Your truth and guiding my thoughts, words, and actions through Your Word and Your Spirit.

Divine Timing

"For the Holy Spirit will teach you
at that time what needs to be said."
Luke 12:12

You promised Your disciples that the Holy Spirit would give them the right words to speak at the exact time they needed them. Lord, there are times when fear and doubt rise up within me, and other times when You give me opportunities to share with others the true reason for my hope. Thank You for speaking to my spirit and bringing Your truths to my mind when I need it most. Thank You for giving me the right words when You prompt me to share Your hope with others, and for bringing Your specific promises to mind when I need Your comfort. Thank You for Your perfect timing.

Divine Truth

With Christ as my witness, I speak with utter truthfulness.
My conscience and the Holy Spirit confirm it.
ROMANS 9:1

Thank You, Father, for the gift of my conscience that helps me to discern right from wrong and good from evil. Lord, there are many complementary approaches I may encounter in my journey toward healing and wellness. Please protect me and give me Your discernment! I want to seek guidance, direction, and comfort from no spirit other than Your Holy Spirit. Help me to know when I'm moving in the wrong direction by giving me a *check*, or a feeling of uneasiness in my spirit. Help me to surrender fully to Your control so I can trust my decisions, actions, and behaviors line up with Yours.

No Escape

I can never escape from your Spirit! I can never get away from your
presence! If I go up to heaven, you are there; if I go down to the grave,
you are there. If I ride the wings of the morning, if I dwell by
the farthest oceans, even there your hand will guide me,
and your strength will support me.
PSALM 139:7–10

God, You are present everywhere I go! No matter what happens or how far I stray from You, You are there. Even when I'm angry and I push You away from me, You never leave me. There is nothing I can ever do and nothing I can leave undone that can separate me from Your love. Thank You that I can never hide from Your comforting presence that dwells within me. Thank You for Your hand that guides me and Your strength that supports me. There is no escape from Your Spirit!

Chapter 10: His Power

Totally Unlimited

*Then, what looked like flames or tongues of fire appeared and settled
on each of them. And everyone present was filled with the
Holy Spirit and began speaking in other languages,
as the Holy Spirit gave them this ability.*
ACTS 2:3–4

Beloved, when My Spirit came to live in you, I no longer needed a physical dwelling place on earth. You became My temple (1 Corinthians 6:19)! The same power that raised Me from the dead took up residence within you (Romans 8:11). If you choose to come under My authority, My Spirit gives you access to all the powers of heaven and earth. But you can't submit to Me while you continue to follow the ways of the world. Lay everything aside to follow Me, and My Spirit will release My power into you. My Spirit will renew, reeducate, and redirect your mind and reveal My truth through My Word.

My child, there is so much more than reading your Bible and knowing in your mind that My Spirit dwells in you. *Experiencing* the scripture through the power of My Spirit makes My Word come alive and My promises real for all you face today. I have so much more in store for you! I want you to live in the fullness of My power within you. I want to ignite that Holy Spirit pilot light I placed in you when you first believed until it is a raging fire that burns within you! Child, I want you to ask for more!

It can be powerful when My Spirit comes upon you. When I came to My followers at Pentecost, the heavens roared and tongues of fire settled on each of them giving them the ability to speak in other languages. When the believers asked Me to send My healing power, the building shook, and they preached My message with boldness (Acts 4:30–31). I can pour out My Spirit with such power that your knees might buckle. You might find yourself resting in a prone position overwhelmed by My love. Or you could experience a pleasant warmth, flush, tingling, or an overwhelming sense of peace. You might be profoundly moved by the power of My Spirit when others lay hands on you, anoint you with oil, and pray for healing (Mark 16:18; James 5:14). As I guide their prayers, you may feel My Spirit stir within you as their words reach the deepest places in your heart. Everyone is unique. There is no right or wrong way to receive and experience My power, but there is no mistaking My Spirit when He comes upon you.

Yes, beloved. I have hardwired into your heart a deep longing for Me that only My Spirit can fill. It was all part of My plan to live in intimacy with you. But living in this world with all its stresses and strains can cause you to leak! Just as I went to the hills to rest and refill, you must set aside time to do the same. Find a quiet place with no worldly distractions and invite My Spirit to come. Surrender your thoughts to Me and give Me permission to come upon you. Rest in My presence and let Me lift your burdens (Matthew 11:28–30). Let Me refill you with the power of My Spirit.

My child, you have all the powers of heaven and earth at your disposal. I am partnering with the medical and faith communities to heal and restore your body, soul, and spirit. But your doctors are limited by human knowledge and wisdom. Their treatments are limited by their capacity to work physiologically in the human body. Dear one, you must never forget: My power is totally unlimited.

PRAY

Resurrection Power

The Spirit of God, who raised Jesus from the dead, lives in you.
And just as God raised Christ Jesus from the dead, he will give life
to your mortal bodies by this same Spirit living within you.
Romans 8:11

Lord, when I think that the same power that raised You from the dead lives inside of me, I can scarce take it in. When I am in alignment with You, surrendering to Your leadership and living by Your terms instead of mine, Your power enables me to do what I can't do on my own. It helps me see beyond my circumstances and find joy and peace in the midst of my pain. Lord, there is always death before a resurrection. Help me to die every day to Your control! Your Spirit is my power source, the very source of life itself!

Power Within

Don't you realize that your body is the temple of the Holy Spirit,
who lives in you and was given to you by God?
You do not belong to yourself.
1 Corinthians 6:19

God, You no longer need to dwell in a physical temple like You did in the Old Testament. Now You make your earthly home in all believers. Thank You for making Your home in me! My body is Your temple, Lord. It belongs to You, and You paid a very high price for it. Lord, help me to honor You with my body. Help me to be a good steward of this physical body You have given me to live in while I am here on this earth. Lord, the enemy has invaded Your temple, and it's time to take back control of Your property. Evict this cancer now, in Jesus' name!

Baptism with Fire

*"I baptize with water those who repent of their sins and turn to God.
But someone is coming soon who is greater than I am—so much greater
that I'm not worthy even to be his slave and carry his sandals.
He will baptize you with the Holy Spirit and with fire."*
MATTHEW 3:11

Jesus, Your cousin John baptized people with water when they repented of their sins. Their baptism was an outward sign of their commitment to turn back to You and follow Your ways. But You, Lord, baptized with fire! You gave them the inward power necessary to carry out their commitment to a changed life! Lord, only by Your Spirit can I do what You call me to do and be who You created me to be. Change me, Lord! Change me from the inside with Your Holy Spirit's power. Let Your fire fall on me!

Ask for More

*While Apollos was in Corinth, Paul traveled through the interior
regions until he reached Ephesus, on the coast, where he found
several believers. "Did you receive the Holy Spirit when
you believed?" he asked them. "No," they replied,
"we haven't even heard that there is a Holy Spirit."*
ACTS 19:1–2

It seems many believers today have also received the gift of forgiveness without knowing the power You gave them to walk in the fullness of their salvation. Lord, help me truly understand the work of the Holy Spirit in Your ministry and message while You were here on earth. Lord, You didn't intend for Your Church to be a set of ideals and doctrines without power. I need Your Spirit to drive my actions and give me the power to live out Your standard for right living. Lord, I want more!

Be Filled

*Don't be drunk with wine, because that will ruin your life.
Instead, be filled with the Holy Spirit, singing psalms
and hymns and spiritual songs among yourselves,
and making music to the Lord in your hearts.*
Ephesians 5:18–19

Being drunk with wine symbolizes the emptiness of my old way of life. But my new life in You promises an indescribable everlasting joy! Rather than yielding to the pleasures of the world to satisfy my needs and desires, Your Spirit can cure my sadness, relieve my stress, and comfort me in all my circumstances. Lord, with Your Spirit in me, I can live supernaturally, singing songs of joy and making music in my heart! Help me to draw constantly on Your power. When I'm running on empty, fill me up again!

Spirit and Life

*"The Spirit alone gives eternal life. Human effort accomplishes nothing.
And the very words I have spoken to you are spirit and life."*
John 6:63

Lord, Your Spirit is the power behind Your promise of eternal life. My human effort to win Your favor and walk in righteousness accomplishes absolutely nothing, Lord. It is only by Your Spirit that I understand my need for You. You have created a hunger in me that only You can satisfy. Lord, You live in me! Reveal Your truth and give me the power to respond. Your very words are spirit and life.

Do Not Stifle

Do not stifle the Holy Spirit.
1 Thessalonians 5:19

Your gifts of prophecy, speaking in tongues, and even healing can be controversial in some of our churches, Father, especially where the Holy Spirit has been stifled. Forgive me when I have avoided, ignored, or tossed aside the presence and gifts of Your Spirit out of fear it might be uncomfortable, messy, or unpredictable. Lord, in my church and others in my community, I pray for the full expression of Your Spirit and gifts to benefit Your entire body!

Power of His Gifts

There are different kinds of spiritual gifts,
but the same Spirit is the source of them all.
1 Corinthians 12:4

Lord, thank You for releasing Your power through Your gifts of special wisdom, knowledge, faith, healing, miracles, prophecy, discernment, and speaking and interpreting tongues! Your Spirit is the source of all these gifts, whether given for a special purpose or given in unusual measure for a specific ministry calling. Lord, thank You that all these gifts work together to make up Your body as a whole. Thank You especially for the gift of healing, and for making a way for Your healing power to be released.

Power of Prayer

*Are any of you sick? You should call for the elders of the church to come
and pray over you, anointing you with oil in the name of the Lord.
Such a prayer offered in faith will heal the sick, and the Lord will make
you well. And if you have committed any sins, you will be forgiven.*
James 5:14–15

You have given clear instructions for believers who fall sick and
how the Church should care for them. Thank You for releasing
Your healing power through the prayer of faith and anointing with
oil. Lord, in Your scriptures, You are the Healer, and prayer is part
of the healing process. Oil symbolized the Holy Spirit and was also
used for medical purposes. Lord, I am sick and I need You to make
me well! Please guide me to leaders and elders who will pray in
faith and anoint me with oil in obedience to this mandate!

Power of Faith

*"I tell you the truth, you can say to this mountain, 'May you be lifted up
and thrown into the sea,' and it will happen. But you must really believe
it will happen and have no doubt in your heart. I tell you, you can pray
for anything, and if you believe that you've received it, it will be yours."*
Mark 11:23–24

You've given believers the gift of faith that releases Your power to
move mountains and do what is impossible for man! Forgive me
when I insist on receiving answers to my prayers before I believe.
Help me to pray expectantly and believe before I receive! Please
reveal any bitterness or selfish motives that may hinder my prayer
life. Help me to pray in alignment with Your will. Most important,
Lord, please help me to focus more on wanting You than what I
need from You!

Power of Agreement

"I also tell you this: If two of you agree here on earth concerning
anything you ask, my Father in heaven will do it for you.
For where two or three gather together as my
followers, I am there among them."
MATTHEW 18:19–20

Thank You, Lord, for Your promise that agreement in prayer between me and another believer releases Your power to answer on my behalf! Lord, lead me to other faith-filled believers who will come alongside me and agree with me in prayer. Together, help us to seek Your Word and pray in accordance with Your will. Holy Spirit, release Your power through our prayers of agreement!

⁓

Power in His Name

"Through faith in the name of Jesus, this man was healed—
and you know how crippled he was before. Faith in Jesus'
name has healed him before your very eyes."
ACTS 3:16

Lord, faith in Your name releases the power of the Spirit to heal and restore. When You walked on earth, a man's name stood for his authority and power to act. By praying in Your name, Peter demonstrated it was You who gave him the power and authority to heal. He wanted to make sure the crowd knew it was You alone who healed the crippled man through faith. Lord, help me to use Your name in faith. In the name of Jesus, release Your power to heal me!

Power to Witness

"But you will receive power when the Holy Spirit comes upon you.
And you will be my witnesses, telling people about me everywhere—
in Jerusalem, throughout Judea, in Samaria,
and to the ends of the earth."
Acts 1:8

Lord, in addition to accessing power beyond the natural through Your Spirit, You give me the courage, boldness, confidence, and authority to be Your witness! Thank You for the mission You have given me to accomplish while I am here on this earth. Lord, give me the power to testify to Your faithfulness! Give me the boldness to share the true reason for my hope. Lord, please give me opportunities to tell the world what You have done for me! Help me to use this cancer for Your glory and purposes!

Power to Bless

"Whoever believes in me, as Scripture has said, rivers of living water
will flow from within them." By this he meant the Spirit, whom those
who believed in him were later to receive. Up to that time the Spirit
had not been given, since Jesus had not yet been glorified.
John 7:38–39 niv

Thank You, Father, for the gift of the Holy Spirit to those who believe in You! Please help me to pour out the same blessing You have given me to those around me. Lord, thank You that Your Spirit flows out of me like rivers of living water to bless and comfort all those You put in my path. Lord, I am not only a conduit for Your power to flow through. I am privileged to carry the presence of the God of the universe into the world! I carry the power to bless. Praise You, Lord!

Chapter 11: His Grace

My Grace Is Enough

Each time he said, "My grace is all you need. My power works best in weakness." So now I am glad to boast about my weaknesses, so that the power of Christ can work through me.
2 CORINTHIANS 12:9

My child, I know you still wonder why. How could this happen to you when you have been working so hard at being good, serving others, and following the rules? You look around you and so many others have done far less, and yet everything seems to be going well for them. You may be tempted to compare your life with theirs, either to rationalize your own faithfulness, or to question My justice. Beloved, be careful not to elevate your own human understanding of justice and fairness higher than Mine, and then desire that I meet your standard. I *am* the standard, and I am a just God, regardless of whether you understand. While on this earth, your human mind will never fully understand why bad things happen to good people. My child, rest assured that I know firsthand your pain and disappointment (Hebrews 2:17–18). I will never leave your side (Matthew 28:20). Take comfort in knowing My grace is all you need.

What is this amazing grace? It is My unmerited favor toward you—the unearned, undeserved gifts I pour out on you. My grace gives you the power to do what you can't do on your own. It gives you the power to face the inevitable trials you will face in this world. Yes, I will give you the grace you need to walk through this valley of cancer. My grace is a free gift to all who seek it, regardless of what they have done or left undone (Ephesians 2:8–9). Dear one, you can't earn your way into a problem-free life. How would you ever know when you've done enough or been good enough? No amount of personal goodness will ever bridge the gap between the world's imperfection and My perfection.

No beloved, you did not deserve this cancer. But only by My abundant grace do you receive one blessing after another (John 1:16). I am the God who made the earth and all the people who live in it. With My hands I stretched out the heavens and commanded the stars in the skies. Your very breath depends on the life I breathed into you (Genesis 2:7; Job 33:4). If I were to take back My Spirit and withdraw My breath, all humanity would turn to dust (Job 34:14–15)! I don't, because of My extravagant and passionate love for all My creation. My child, nothing, not all powers of heaven or hell, can ever keep Me from loving you (Romans 8:38–39).

Dear one, please know this: it was by My grace that you woke up every day before this diagnosis. And it will be by My grace you wake up every day after. For in Me, you live and move and have your very being (Acts 17:28). My grace saved you from destruction and promises a life of abundance in this world and the next. You may be pressed on every side by troubles, but you will never be crushed and broken. You may be confused and under attack, but I will never abandon you. You may fall down, but you will get up again and keep on going (2 Corinthians 4:8–9). Because My grace is enough for you. My power works best in your weakness.

PRAY

Grace upon Grace

Out of his fullness we have all received grace in place of grace
already given. For the law was given through Moses;
grace and truth came through Jesus Christ.
JOHN 1:16–17 NIV

Lord, You revealed Your nature and Your will to Your servant Moses. Through the law, You showed us how to live while here on this earth. Then You came in the flesh to fulfill Your law. You gave us the power to live according to Your will through Your Spirit, and Your abundant grace when we fall short. Lord, thank You for love, forgiveness, healing, and restoration. Thank You for Your rich blessings, one abundant blessing after another, grace upon grace!

Freedom by Grace

He is so rich in kindness and grace that he purchased our freedom
with the blood of his Son and forgave our sins.
EPHESIANS 1:7

You paid the full price for my freedom. Before, I was a slave to sin and burdened by rules I could never follow. No amount of intellectual, moral, or religious effort could have saved me. But Your blood set me free! You redeemed me from a debt I could never pay. Lord, I will never fully understand the cost of nailing my sin upon that cross. Thank You for the priceless gift of grace. Help me never to forget.

Free and Undeserved

*And since it is through God's kindness, then it is not by
their good works. For in that case, God's grace would
not be what it really is—free and undeserved.*
ROMANS 11:6

You didn't choose to love me because I deserved it, Father. You chose
to love me because it is Your nature to love and cherish Your creation.
Lord, thank You for loving me unconditionally, regardless of what
I've done or left undone! Give me understanding of what Your grace
really is—full and undeserved. I can't earn my way into Your favor. I
can only accept Your grace with thankfulness and praise. Forgive me
when I ask You why. I don't need to know. I only need to know You.

Abundant Grace

*The grace of our Lord was poured out on me abundantly,
along with the faith and love that are in Christ Jesus.*
1 TIMOTHY 1:14 NIV

You poured out Your grace on me so abundantly, Lord. Thank You
for the outpouring of faith and love that is in Christ Jesus. Lord, I
want more of You! Please use this cancer to draw me close to Your
heart so my relationship with You grows deeper and deeper. Help
me to love as You love and to stand in faith for my healing.

Restored by Grace

And the God of all grace, who called you to his eternal glory in Christ,
after you have suffered a little while, will himself restore
you and make you strong, firm and steadfast.
1 Peter 5:10 niv

Lord, when I view eternity as an infinite line, I know my life on earth is but a dot on the line of time. While it feels like it will last forever, in the perspective of eternity, this cancer journey will only last "a little while." Lord, thank You that all suffering, including cancer, will be removed for all eternity when there will be no more death or sorrow or crying or pain. Lord, by Your grace, I pray You will remove this cancer from me now while I am still here on this earth. Lord, make me strong, firm, and steadfast. Heal me, Lord, all for Your glory.

Strength through Grace

Timothy, my dear son, be strong through
the grace that God gives you in Christ Jesus.
2 Timothy 2:1

Your saving grace astonishes me! Just as I am saved by Your grace alone, I must live every day by Your grace alone. Lord, help me to trust completely in You and live in Your grace. Forgive me when I try to live for You in my own power. By Your grace, I receive Your supernatural strength to face each day. Please, Lord, help me be strong! Give me Your strength to navigate through the trials and challenges of this life. Give me the grace I need to walk through this cancer.

Throne of Grace

So let us come boldly to the throne of our gracious God.
There we will receive his mercy, and we will find
grace to help us when we need it most.
Hebrews 4:16

Lord, instead of praying through a priest or mediator, Your death and resurrection made it possible for me to come directly into Your throne room with bold assurance! You are my friend and counselor, Lord. I can approach You with my head held high and trust You will give me grace to meet my needs. Yet, I know this privilege came at a very high price, bought and paid for by Your blood. Help me never to forget that when I pray, I stand on holy ground. I come into Your throne room with humble reverence, knowing I stand in the presence of the King.

Grace to Heal

Stephen, a man full of God's grace and power,
performed amazing miracles and signs among the people.
Acts 6:8

By the power of Your Spirit, Lord, You gave Stephen the grace to perform amazing miracles and signs among the people. Thank You that the same grace is available to believers today. Lord, please give me the grace to exercise the gifts You have given me. Lead me to others who believe in Your grace to heal the sick. By Your healing grace, make me whole again!

Steward His Grace

Each of you should use whatever gift you have received to serve others, as faithful stewards of God's grace in its various forms.
1 PETER 4:10 NIV

You have given me good gifts by Your grace. Forgive me for holding back and believing I have nothing to offer, or for turning inward and focusing all my attention on myself. Lord, show me the gifts that I carry. Even in this time of personal trial, show me ways to use my gifts to serve You and to bless others, whether encouraging those going through a similar journey, or simply praying for them in silence in a clinic waiting room. Lord, break my heart for the things that break Yours. Help me to keep You in the center of this battle. Lord, thank You for grace.

Grace Rules

So just as sin ruled over all people and brought them to death, now God's wonderful grace rules instead, giving us right standing with God and resulting in eternal life through Jesus Christ our Lord.
ROMANS 5:21

God, Your wonderful grace rules over my body, soul, and spirit—over every aspect of my life! Remind me that I am always in right standing with You, even when I fail or fall short. Lord, condemnation is not from You. Guilt, shame, doubt, and fear are lies of the enemy who wants to steal, kill, and destroy. Thank You that You came to save the world, not condemn it. Because Your grace rules, I am free!

Grace to the Humble

And he gives grace generously. As the Scriptures say,
"God opposes the proud but gives grace to the humble."
JAMES 4:6

Lord, thank You for grace to stand against my own worldly desires. Pride and self-sufficiency lead me to believe that I deserve all I can see, touch, and imagine. Lord, by grace alone, I am worthy of Your unconditional love. Help me to surrender, Lord. Help me to recognize that I am nothing without You. The only thing that can fill the deep longing in my heart is You. You are all I need. You complete me.

Mere Mortals

What are mere mortals that you should think about them,
human beings that you should care for them?
PSALM 8:4

When I look up at the heavens You created, God, I am overwhelmed by Your majesty! You created the universe and all the galaxies, yet You came to earth as a human being to save the world! How can You care for a people who constantly disappoint You and drift away from You, even though You never leave or forsake them? But Lord, in spite of these things, even though I am a tiny speck in the vast heavens, a mere mortal, I am of great value to You. I am of such value that You would have bled and died just for me. I bear the stamp of the Creator of the universe. I am Yours. Every breath and every heartbeat is by Your grace alone.

Poor in Spirit

"God blesses those who are poor and realize their need for him,
for the Kingdom of Heaven is theirs."
MATTHEW 5:3

Lord, this cancer has taken me to the end of my own strength and abilities. I am poor in spirit and I have nowhere else to turn. My strength is gone, and I am fully dependent on You. I need You, Lord! Thank You for taking my hand and leading me into a deep level of grace I could never find on my own power. Your grace is enough, Lord. When I am weak, You are strong.

Testify to His Grace

But my life is worth nothing to me unless I use it for finishing the work
assigned me by the Lord Jesus—the work of telling others the
Good News about the wonderful grace of God.
ACTS 20:24

My life is worth nothing unless I use it for Your glory. Lord, please take what the enemy is using for evil—this cancer—and turn it into something good! Let me be a testimony to others of Your power and Your promises, and let me start now—whether at the doctor's office, during treatments, or with family and friends, give me boldness to share Your message of hope. Help me tell others the Good News of Your wonderful grace!

Chapter 12: His Mercy

A Fresh Start

~~~

Great is his faithfulness;
his mercies begin afresh each morning.
LAMENTATIONS 3:23

My child, while My *grace* is behind every blessing, it is My *mercy* that prevents Me from penalizing your every mistake. Right now, you may think I am withholding My mercy. It may seem your prayers are not being answered in the ways you would hope. Beloved, I am not using cancer as a way of punishing you for not praying enough, not reading your Bible enough, or because you think you are a disappointment to Me. I don't use illness to teach you a lesson, to get even, or to get your attention. It is not in My character to treat you this way. Remember, I came to save the world, not to judge it (John 3:17). There is no condemnation in Me, and no mistake you could ever make can keep Me from loving you (Romans 8:1, 38–39). It is impossible for Me to punish you because I already took the punishment for you.

Dear one, consider My chosen one, King David. He may have been well known as a shepherd, giant-killer, poet, and mighty warrior, but he was also an adulterer and murderer. David was quick to confess his sin, and his repentance was genuine. I forgave him and showed him mercy, and even referred to him as a "man after my own heart" (Acts 13:22). He never took My mercy lightly or My blessings for granted. He praised Me even with his enemies in relentless pursuit. Without mercy, My servant Paul would never have become the greatest faith hero in history. He hunted and murdered Christians before he met Me. Paul called himself the worst sinner of all, yet he never forgot he was saved by grace and that I used him as a prime example of My great mercy (1 Timothy 1:13–16).

Remember My parable of the prodigal son? After squandering all of his inheritance on wild living, he was so poor and hungry he was forced to eat with the pigs. When he finally came to his senses, he returned home to his father to ask forgiveness and offer his services as a hired hand. His father ran to meet him with open arms, dressed him in fine clothing, and threw a party to celebrate his safe return. In spite of all he had done, his father showed him mercy and never once rejected him as a son (Luke 15:11–32).

My child, your relationship with Me can be much the same. You may not murder, commit adultery, or squander an inheritance on wild living, but every day you will encounter opportunities to fall short. You may lose your patience, get angry, doubt Me, neglect Me, and even push Me away. You might even find yourself eating with the pigs (Romans 8:5–6). But child, while you may drift away from Me, My relationship with you never changes. My tender mercies start fresh every morning. You can never lose your identity as My child (Galatians 3:26). My love and mercy will reach out and welcome you home, regardless of what you've done, where you've been, or how long you've been gone. I paid with My blood for your right to live in My presence (Hebrews 4:15–16). Beloved, you are worthy because every day I make you worthy. Today is a new day, and it's time for a fresh start. It's time for a party.

PRAY

Whiter Than Snow

Have mercy on me, O God, because of your unfailing love. Because of your great compassion, blot out the stain of my sins. Wash me clean from my guilt. Purify me from my sin. . . . Purify me from my sins, and I will be clean; wash me, and I will be whiter than snow.
Psalm 51:1–2, 7

When David committed adultery with Bathsheba and murdered her husband to cover up his transgression, he was deeply sorry and cried out to You for Your mercy. But even sins as serious as these were not outside Your outstretched arms of forgiveness. I, too, have made many mistakes, Lord. Have mercy on me! Restore me from the inside out so Your desires become mine. Wash me clean from any guilt I may be carrying. Purify me! Thank You for making me whiter than snow.

Forgiven and Forgotten

The LORD is compassionate and merciful, slow to get angry and filled with unfailing love. He will not constantly accuse us, nor remain angry forever. He does not punish us for all our sins; he does not deal harshly with us, as we deserve. For his unfailing love toward those who fear him is as great as the height of the heavens above the earth. He has removed our sins as far from us as the east is from the west.
Psalm 103:8–12

Just as the east and west can never meet, that is the distance You separate my sin from me. Thank You that you never remember my mistakes after I confess them to You and ask Your forgiveness. Lord, help me when I carry guilt and shame over my past transgressions, even after You have forgotten them. Forgive me for believing Your blood isn't enough to wash me clean. I'm so sorry for believing You may be using my past mistakes to punish me. Even when I must endure the natural consequences of my transgressions, I know You are with me and will never leave me. Thank You, Lord. By Your mercy, my past mistakes are truly forgiven and forgotten.

Back Home

"For if you return to the LORD, your relatives and your children will be treated mercifully by their captors, and they will be able to return to this land. For the LORD your God is gracious and merciful. If you return to him, he will not continue to turn his face from you."
2 Chronicles 30:9

Lord, throughout a history of good kings and bad kings, Your people rebelled and turned their backs on You. But in Your mercy, You always welcomed them back home. In this scripture, King Hezekiah sent letters throughout Judah and Israel promising all who returned to You would be treated mercifully. Lord, I may have drifted away from You, but today, I come home. Thank You for not turning Your face from me! I yield my body, mind, will, and emotions to Your care and control!

Mercies from Heaven

"But as soon as they were at peace, your people again committed evil in your sight, and once more you let their enemies conquer them. Yet whenever your people turned and cried to you again for help, you listened once more from heaven. In your wonderful mercy, you rescued them many times!"
Nehemiah 9:28

I take great comfort in knowing that You always hear my cries for help from heaven. Forgive me for allowing myself to get caught up in the cares and concerns of this world, for investing my time and attention in everything but You. My enemy is relentless, Lord. Please don't let this cancer conquer me! Rescue me again from the enemy's grip! I turn to You alone, Lord. I cry out to You for help! Once again, show me Your wonderful mercy!

Mercy for the Desperate

"I'm in a desperate situation!" David replied to Gad.
"But let us fall into the hands of the Lord, for his mercy is great.
Do not let me fall into human hands."
2 Samuel 24:14

Lord, I have followed my own path for far too long, and I have trusted in the world's ways before Your ways. You have often been an afterthought in this journey. But You, Lord, are the only one who can save me. Forgive me for putting all my trust in human hands. Forgive me for trying to control every detail of my life when truly, I have no control. Like David, my situation is desperate. But even then, Your justice is perfect. I am at Your mercy, Lord. I surrender my life to You. I surrender this cancer to You. I am Yours. Thank You for Your great mercy toward me. I fall into Your hands.

Mercy for the Anguished

I will be glad and rejoice in your unfailing love, for you have seen my
troubles, and you care about the anguish of my soul. You have not
handed me over to my enemies but have set me in a safe place.
Have mercy on me, Lord, for I am in distress. Tears blur my
eyes. My body and soul are withering away.
Psalm 31:7–9

Yes, Lord, my soul is anguished and I am in distress! Tears blur my eyes, and sometimes it feels like my body and soul are withering away. Lord, thank You for not handing me over to this cancer and for setting me in a safe place. Lord, I rejoice in Your unfailing love, for You have seen my troubles! Thank You for caring about the anguish of my soul. Have mercy on me, Lord! In Your mercy, restore my health!

Saved by Mercy

When God our Savior revealed his kindness and love,
he saved us, not because of the righteous things we had done,
but because of his mercy. He washed away our sins,
giving us a new birth and new life through the Holy Spirit.
TITUS 3:4–5

You reveal Your kindness and love by washing away my sin and giving me a new life in the Spirit. Help me to always remember it was never about the things I've done or left undone, but because of Your mercy. As I grow in this new life with You, Your tender mercies start fresh every day. Thank You for the redemptive work of the Son, the forgiveness of the Father, and the gift of the Holy Spirit who washes away my sin and continually renews my heart and mind to make me more like You.

What He Requires

No, O people, the LORD has told you what is good, and this is
what he requires of you: to do what is right, to love mercy,
and to walk humbly with your God.
MICAH 6:8

Lord, there is no mystery in what You expect from me. You have given clear directions of what You require of Your followers. By the power of Your Spirit, help me to always do what is right. Help me to show others the same mercy You have shown to me. Finally, help me walk humbly with You, always remembering that I am nothing without You.

HOPE IN HIS MERCY

*He does not delight in the strength of the horse; He takes no pleasure
in the legs of a man. The LORD takes pleasure in those
who fear Him, in those who hope in His mercy.*
PSALM 147:10–11 NKJV

Forgive me when I find myself trusting the doctors, their treatments, and my own resilience more than I trust You. There is nothing wrong with medical professionals using their gifts and my own determination carrying me through this journey. But their healing gifts and my strength without Your power behind it are worth little. You do not delight in their strength or mine, Lord. Both come directly from You. I put my hope in Your mercy alone. All for Your glory.

HELD BY MERCY

*Unless the LORD had been my help, my soul would soon have settled
in silence. If I say, "My foot slips," Your mercy, O LORD, will hold me up.*
PSALM 94:17–18 NKJV

Without Your help, Father, through this cancer diagnosis, I would be completely lost. I can't imagine going through this journey without You. Indeed, my soul would be settled in silence as dead. But Lord, You hear my cries for mercy! When my foot slips, You catch me. When doubt fills my mind, Your comforting presence renews my hope. Thank You, Lord. Your mercy lifts me high. I am held by Your mercy alone.

Chapter 13: His Voice

A Gentle Whisper

❧

My sheep listen to my voice; I know them,
and they follow me.
JOHN 10:27

My child, I know you are desperate to hear My voice. There are too many questions and too many uncertainties. When you need wisdom, you need simply ask Me (James 1:4–5). I created you to hear My voice, and I speak to you through My Spirit when you stay connected to Me through prayer and My Word. Prayer is not you bringing Me a shopping list of petitions, but a two-way conversation like you would have with a friend. When you come to Me in prayer and wait for Me to respond, I can speak to you through that same gentle whisper I spoke to My prophet Elijah (1 Kings 19:11–12). But you must get into position to hear My voice by removing the distractions. When you wait quietly before Me, My Spirit speaks to your spirit, your spirit speaks My message to your mind, and your mind eventually hears My voice and knows what to do.

Beloved, turn your worries into prayers and tell Me everything you need (Philippians 4:6). Tell Me every detail (Psalm 37:23). Don't give up when you can't hear My voice or the answers come slowly. Persistent prayer proves your faith in Me. Believe Me when I tell you that everyone who asks, receives; everyone who seeks, finds; and the door is opened to everyone who knocks (Matthew 7:7–8). Even in the silence, I am working on your behalf because I am always on your side (Romans 8:31). I make all things work together for good when you love Me and are called to My purpose (Romans 8:28). I will surely give justice to My chosen ones who press into Me with shameless persistence (Luke 11:6–8).

Listen for My voice through the power of My Word (Hebrews 4:12)! When you read the scriptures, My Spirit brings the words to life and makes the Word personal to your specific needs and prayers. I can speak through verses you may have read countless times in the past, bringing fresh revelation to your current dilemma. There is not one feeling or emotion, not one situation you will ever experience, that My Word does not address. Through it, I speak hope into your suffering and your deepest sorrows.

But there are other ways to hear My voice. Sometimes I'll speak through prophecy to edify, encourage, and comfort you (Romans 12:6; 1 Corinthians 14:3). If someone claims to have a word from Me about your situation, be sure to test that word against scripture (1 Thessalonians 5:20–21). Sometimes I'll speak to you in dreams and visions (Genesis 28:11–19; Genesis 37:5–11; Acts 2:17). Always ask Me to make sure that any prophetic word, dream, or vision you receive is truly from Me (1 John 4:1–2). And while I may speak to you through wise people, be sure to consult with Me first. Never seek counsel from the ungodly (Psalm 1:1–3), and never view the counsel of man as the final authority (Romans 15:14). In all circumstances, seek confirmation through the Word and prayer.

My child, I have given you a sound mind to make decisions (2 Timothy 1:7). Through My Spirit and the Word, you can know My thoughts, talk to Me, and expect Me to answer. If you must move forward without clear confirmation, trust that I will close doors or speak to your spirit, giving you a persistent uneasiness if you're headed off course. My sheep do hear my voice, and they follow Me. Listen for My gentle whisper.

PRAY

Ask, Seek, and Knock

"So I say to you: Ask and it will be given to you; seek and you
will find; knock and the door will be opened to you.
For everyone who asks receives; the one who seeks finds;
and to the one who knocks, the door will be opened."
LUKE 11:9–10 NIV

I can hardly fathom that the Creator of the entire universe wants to have a two-way conversation with me! Thank You that You hear me when I speak to You, and You are eager to answer. Lord, forgive me when I pray a few times and give up because the answers don't come according to my time frame. I'm sorry when I assume You don't hear me or the answer is no. Please, Lord. Give me faith to persist! Give me focus to keep my eyes on You. Help me to persist in my prayer life and not give up! I want more, Lord. More of Your love, wisdom, knowledge, and peace!

Ask for Anything

But if you remain in me and my words remain in you,
you may ask for anything you want, and it will be granted!
JOHN 15:7

Jesus, You spent time with Your disciples and called them friends. As friends, You confided in them about everything Your Father told You. Lord, I want this same kind of personal relationship with You. I want to be Your friend, have deep conversations with You, and learn to know Your heart! Help me to stay close to You in thought, Word, and prayer as a branch is attached to the vine. In this place of deep intimacy, where I remain in You and Your words remain in me, I can ask for anything and it will be granted!

ASK FOR WISDOM

If you need wisdom, ask our generous God, and he will give it to you.
He will not rebuke you for asking. But when you ask him, be sure that
your faith is in God alone. Do not waver, for a person with
divided loyalty is as unsettled as a wave of the
sea that is blown and tossed by the wind.
JAMES 1:5–6

I need more than knowledge, Lord. I need Your divine wisdom to make the right decisions! There are so many options I must consider and so many decisions to make! But Lord, You promise to give me wisdom when I ask. Thank You that I don't have to stumble around in the darkness hoping to find my way. Lord, I fully expect You will hear me and answer me when I pray. Help me not to doubt. Help me not to waver. Lord, I come to You first. Your voice is not just another voice among many to consider, but the *only* voice that truly matters. Thank You for guiding my choices!

⁓

ASK PERSISTENTLY

And will not God bring about justice for his chosen ones,
who cry out to him day and night? Will he keep putting them off?
LUKE 18:7 NIV

Lord, I'll be honest. Sometimes it feels like my prayers are bouncing off the ceiling. Do You really hear me? I am waiting for You to speak, Lord. I am waiting for You to rise up and meet my needs! Help me to trust You hear my calls for help! Help me to press in and persist in my conversations with You, even through the silence. Help me to trust You are answering my prayers even when nothing appears to be happening. I cry out to You day and night, Lord. I am desperate to hear Your voice! Help me to trust in Your perfect timing. Please, give me the strength to pray with persistence until the answers come.

Ask with a Pure Heart

Yet you don't have what you want because you don't ask God for it.
And even when you ask, you don't get it because your motives are
all wrong—you want only what will give you pleasure.
JAMES 4:2–3

Forgive me, Father, when I assume You have more important matters to deal with than talking to me and hearing about my problems. Thank You that You are not a God of scarcity, but a God of infinite abundance! You are not limited to reserving Your time and attention for only the most urgent requests. There is more than enough of You to go around! Lord, I am worthy to converse with You in prayer and hear Your voice because You made me worthy! Lord, You made it possible to cast *all* my cares on You. I bring all my needs before You, Lord. Help my prayer life reflect Your heart and Your desires.

⌒

A Gentle Whisper

"Go out and stand before me on the mountain," the LORD told him.
And as Elijah stood there, the LORD passed by, and a mighty windstorm
hit the mountain. It was such a terrible blast that the rocks were torn
loose, but the LORD was not in the wind. After the wind there was an
earthquake, but the LORD was not in the earthquake. And after the
earthquake there was a fire, but the LORD was not in the fire.
And after the fire there was the sound of a gentle whisper.
1 KINGS 19:11–12

Lord, forgive my preconceived notions for how I expect You will make Yourself known to me. In past encounters, You may have appeared to me or others in a certain way. Yes, I may find You in churches, revival meetings, conferences, and in the prayers of powerfully anointed people. But I can also hear You whisper to the quietness of my humble heart. Forgive me when I've set expectations on how and where I will hear Your voice. I don't want to miss You, Lord. Help me to hear Your gentle whisper!

His Word Speaks

The instructions of the LORD are perfect, reviving the soul.
The decrees of the LORD are trustworthy, making wise the simple.
The commandments of the LORD are right, bringing joy to the
heart. The commands of the LORD are clear, giving insight for living.
PSALM 19:7–8

Thank You for the power of Your scriptures, my perfect instruction manual for daily living! Your Word revives me, Lord! It keeps me wise, gives joy to my heart, and light to my eyes. Your Word warns me of pending danger and points me toward the best course of action. But Lord, the Bible is more than a collection of words that guide my actions. Your Spirit within me makes Your Word come to life! Draw me into Your scriptures, Lord! Your timing is perfect, Lord, and there is no such thing as coincidence. When You highlight a specific scripture for a certain circumstance, I can trust Your Spirit is speaking to me!

Seek and Find

In those days when you pray, I will listen.
If you look for me wholeheartedly, you will find me.
JEREMIAH 29:12–13

Father, even in times of deep trouble when Your voice is silent, even then, You have not forgotten me. When I pray, You will listen. When I look for You wholeheartedly, You promise I will find You. Lord, I invite You into this cancer and the challenges I face today. Come, Lord, come! Use this time to draw me close to Your heart. Continue to mold me and shape me into the person You have created me to be. Lord, use this time for Your glory and purposes!

Kingdom Secrets

He replied, "You are permitted to understand the secrets
of the Kingdom of Heaven, but others are not."
Matthew 13:11

Lord, Your disciples came to understand Your deep secrets because they spent quality time with You. They left everything behind to follow You. I, too, want to know Your thoughts and desires! I want to understand the secrets of Your kingdom. Lord, give me eyes to see, ears to hear, and a heart that understands. Please, Lord, I hunger for more! Give me the discipline to set time aside to simply rest in Your presence. Give me the courage to surrender my all. Speak, Lord. Tell me Your secrets!

Just Ask

After this, David asked the Lord, "Should I move back to one of
the towns of Judah?" "Yes," the Lord replied. Then David asked,
"Which town should I go to?" "To Hebron," the Lord answered.
2 Samuel 2:1

I'm amazed at how Your servant David consulted with You on his every move in order to accomplish Your purposes. He interacted with You in two-way conversation as I would seek wise counsel from family members and friends. Lord, even when my next step seems obvious, remind me to always bring it to You for confirmation and further clarity. You alone know my best course of action in this battle to defeat my enemy. I want this level of intimacy with You, Lord. I want to be someone after Your own heart.

Go

But the Lord said, "Go, for Saul is my chosen instrument
to take my message to the Gentiles and to kings,
as well as to the people of Israel."
ACTS 9:15

Lord, You chose Your servant Saul (Paul) to take Your message of hope to Gentiles and kings! But before You spoke to him on the road to Damascus and rendered him blind, he was a persecutor of Christians! Ananias defied all human logic and common sense when You told him to go restore Paul's sight. Once again, Lord, Your voice changed the course of history. You speak to me, too, Lord, and You have a plan and a purpose for me! Open my heart to hear Your commands. Help me to obey when I hear You say, "Go."

⸺

Godly Counsel

The godly offer good counsel; they teach right from wrong.
They have made God's law their own, so they will
never slip from his path.
PSALM 37:30–31

Thank You, God, for the wise men and women You put in my path to speak wisdom into my situation, whether family members, pastors, doctors, or friends. Lord, always remind me to seek truth, wisdom, and guidance from You first as I walk through this valley of cancer. Please put people in my path who will confirm Your truth, and protect me from voices and philosophies of the world that contradict Your Spirit and are not of You. Lord, always remind me to test the counsel of man against Yours. May their words confirm what You have already testified to be true. Lord, please give me courage to move counterintuitively, if necessary, to walk in Your will. Help me to hear Your voice over all the other voices.

Morning by Morning

*The Sovereign L*ORD *has given me his words of wisdom, so that I know how to comfort the weary. Morning by morning he wakens me and opens my understanding to his will. The Sovereign L*ORD *has spoken to me, and I have listened. I have not rebelled or turned away.*
ISAIAH 50:4–5

Lord, thank You that Your words of wisdom can waken me each morning and open my understanding to Your will. Forgive me when the first thoughts that come to my mind upon waking are my worries for tomorrow and to-dos for the day! Lord, bring Your comforting presence to my mind at the first morning light. I will not turn away. Open my ears to hear You speak! Remind me to pray each and every morning: *Thank You for another day, Lord! Thank You for my life! I give You this day, Lord. I give You all my worries, concerns, tasks, and plans! What do You have for me today, Lord? What do You want me to know? I love You, Lord! How can I bring You glory?*

Prophecy, Visions, and Dreams

"'In the last days,' God says, 'I will pour out my Spirit upon all people. Your sons and daughters will prophesy. Your young men will see visions, and your old men will dream dreams.'"
ACTS 2:17

Thank You that I live in the "last days," the time between Your first and second coming. Thank You for the promise that Your Spirit will speak to me through prophecy, visions, and dreams! Lord, please give me an extra measure of discernment when You speak to me through the prophetic word of another believer. Open the eyes of my heart to discern anything You might want to show me through dreams and visions. Please lead me to godly men and women who can help me understand. Show me how to test the spirit to make sure it comes from You and aligns with Your Word. Protect me from false teachers and ungodly spirits, Lord. Help me to trust Your spirit within me to discern Your truth.

Chapter 14: His Faithfulness

The Ultimate Promise Keeper

Let us hold tightly without wavering to the hope we affirm,
for God can be trusted to keep his promise.
HEBREWS 10:23

My child, faith is trusting I am faithful and will do what I say I will do. It is the confident assurance that what you hope for will actually happen (Hebrews 11:1). Oh, so often, My children pray backward! They lift their requests up to Me, and if the answers don't come in the way they expect, they doubt I hear, doubt I care, or even exist at all. But if I answer a desperate prayer, they jump for joy and shout it from the rooftops. *Look what the Lord did! He healed me! Can you believe it?* Beloved, you often receive and *then* you believe. But I want you to believe *first*, and then receive (Matthew 21:22). You must come to Me as little children (Matthew 18:3). Most of My little ones don't jump for joy at their parents' faithfulness. *Look what my mom did! She fed me today. Can you believe it?*

No, My little ones have a pure and simple faith in the responsible adults who care for them. They haven't yet experienced the visible inconsistencies and religious traditions that often cast doubt on your beliefs as an adult. They know by faith I will meet their needs. They won't point out examples of when I didn't. When they are taught the miracles in the Bible, they simply believe. Adults can't help wondering sometimes if biblical miracles are really just stories, and modern-day miracles are really coincidences. Little children don't need to understand all the mysteries of My kingdom and solve all the apparent impossibilities in the material realm in order to have faith. They believe and expect to receive. You must be like these little ones and trust in My promises.

My Word is full of people with childlike faith who believed in My faithfulness and expected to receive. Noah built a huge boat in the middle of dry land to save his family from the flood that destroyed humankind (Hebrews 11:7). Moses forfeited his comfortable position as the Pharaoh's adopted grandson to lead My people out of slavery in Egypt (Hebrews 11:24–27). Abraham, a childless old man, believed My promise to give him a son who would make his descendants as numerous as the stars (Genesis 15:4–5). He never doubted My faithfulness (Romans 4:20–21). Sure enough, when he was one hundred years old, his ninety-year-old wife, Sarah, bore him a son (Genesis 21:1–7).

My child, you may fear you don't have *enough* faith. Maybe you've been told by well-meaning believers if you just had more faith, you would be healed. I'm so sorry if this has been your experience. It's true that I often told people like the hemorrhaging woman (Matthew 9:22), the leper (Luke 17:19), and the blind man (Luke 18:42) that their faith made them well. But I also healed the son of a desperate father who cried out to Me, "I do believe, but help me overcome my unbelief!" Take care not to conclude that *if* people receive healing because of their faith, *then* those who aren't healed don't have enough! You may even know people with no faith at all who receive healing on this earth, and those with unwavering faith whom I heal when I welcome them home. Beloved, it's not up to you to sort all this out, nor should you. You will always encounter mysteries and apparent inconsistencies in your walk with Me. Your faith in Me must never depend on your experiences or your ability to figure Me out. You only need to know I am faithful. You can *always* trust Me to keep My promises.

PRAY

ENDURING FAITHFULNESS

Your faithfulness extends to every generation,
as enduring as the earth you created.
PSALM 119:90

Lord, Your faithfulness extends to every generation! You are as enduring as the earth You created. You were faithful to Your creation through all the generations before me, and You will remain faithful through all the generations after. Lord, You never change! You are the same yesterday, today, and forever. Thank You that I can count on Your promises of healing and restoration through the ages.

PERFECT FAITHFULNESS

He is the Rock; his deeds are perfect. Everything he does is just and fair.
He is a faithful God who does no wrong; how just and upright he is!
DEUTERONOMY 32:4

Lord, You are indeed my Rock. Everything You do is perfect, just, and fair. Even when Your actions seem beyond my human reasoning, You are a faithful God who can do no wrong. Lord, help me to stand on Your promises whether or not everything makes sense around me. I surrender my need to understand. Lord, I choose to trust in Your faithfulness. I choose to trust You.

Believe and Receive

"You can pray for anything, and if you have faith,
you will receive it."
Matthew 21:22

Thank You for the promise that I can pray for anything in faith and receive it! Forgive me when I pray backward, asking without truly believing until I receive what I ask for. Teach me to pray in faith, Lord. Help me to believe before I receive. Help me to believe, even when the answers don't come in the ways I expect them to come. Lord, I understand that my prayers must be aligned with Your will and Your character. You will not grant requests that would not be Your best for me. Lord, use this time in the valley of cancer to draw me close. Reveal Yourself to me through Your Word and Your Spirit. I want to know You, Lord. My heart's desire is for Your plans and mine to be perfectly aligned. I want to pray in faith and fully expect to receive!

Childlike Faith

Then he said, "I tell you the truth, unless you turn from your sins
and become like little children, you will never
get into the Kingdom of Heaven."
Matthew 18:3

Lord, if loving earthly parents faithfully care for their children, how much more will You care for me! Help me to have the heart of a child! Forgive me for doubting Your faithfulness, and for being skeptical and even surprised when something goes my way and You meet my basic needs! Lord, help me to come to You humbly and sincerely, knowing I am dependent on You for my every breath! Help me to trust You, just as small children are fully dependent on loving parents to meet their every need. Help me to trust You without giving it a second thought!

Faithful to the Unfaithful

If we are unfaithful, he remains faithful,
for he cannot deny who he is.
2 Timothy 2:13

You promise to stay at my side when my faith wavers, especially during the times I find myself completely faithless. Lord, forgive me for my anger at You over this cancer. Forgive me for believing You didn't care, You didn't protect me, and that You let me down. I know it is impossible for You to turn Your back on me, even when I turn my back on You. Thank You that You remain faithful, even to the unfaithful.

Faith That Pleases

And it is impossible to please God without faith.
Anyone who wants to come to him must believe that God
exists and that he rewards those who sincerely seek him.
Hebrews 11:6

Lord, I know You want more from me than an acknowledgment of Your existence. Even the devil does that! You want me to seek You with all my heart, soul, mind, and strength. You want a personal relationship with me that will transform my life. Lord, thank You for the promise that You will be found by me. Yes, it pleases You when I act in faith on the knowledge I have today. But I hunger for more! I want to know You, Lord. The more I know You, the more my faith will grow.

Small as a Mustard Seed

The apostles said to the Lord, "Show us how to increase our faith."
The Lord answered, "If you had faith even as small as a mustard seed,
you could say to this mulberry tree, 'May you be uprooted
and be planted in the sea,' and it would obey you!"
LUKE 17:5–6

You said a mustard seed of faith was enough for a tree to be uprooted and thrown into the sea at my command, Lord. A mustard seed is very, very small! But You can do big things with a humble and obedient heart and a small amount of genuine faith! Lord, like the disciples, I want more. But I know the amount of faith I have is not as important as the posture of my heart. Lord, I turn my heart toward You, and I honor Your holy name. Make this mustard seed of faith within me take root and grow! Let it grow until it uproots anything that competes with You in my life.

Help My Unbelief!

Immediately the father of the child cried out
and said with tears, "Lord, I believe; help my unbelief!"
MARK 9:24 NKJV

Father, You don't condemn me when I struggle with unbelief. When this father tearfully confessed his struggle to You, You immediately delivered his son. You knew how desperately he wanted to believe. Lord, I am like this father, I believe. But please, help my unbelief! I know growing in faith is an ongoing process. Help me choose every day to place my trust in You. I can't muster up faith like this on my own power. Only by Your grace can I truly believe nothing is impossible for You.

Desperate Faith

Just then a woman who had suffered for twelve years with constant bleeding came up behind him. She touched the fringe of his robe, for she thought, "If I can just touch his robe, I will be healed." Jesus turned around, and when he saw her he said, "Daughter, be encouraged! Your faith has made you well." And the woman was healed at that moment.

MATTHEW 9:20–22

This woman was so desperate to get well, she had nothing to lose. She broke all the rules of her culture. Her bleeding rendered her untouchable and unclean, forbidden to live a normal life among the people and certainly forbidden to touch a rabbi. Yet she knew if she could just push through the crowds and get close enough to touch the fringe of Your robe, she would be healed. And yes, at her touch, power flowed from You and changed her unchangeable situation. Her desperate faith made her well! I, too, am desperate. I am desperate to touch the fringe of Your robe and desperate to be healed. Lord, please give me faith and boldness like this woman! Change in me what no doctor can change. Heal in me what no doctor can heal. Lord, I want to hear You say, "Be encouraged. Your faith has made you well!"

Faith to Be Healed

Looking straight at him, Paul realized he had faith to be
healed. So Paul called to him in a loud voice, "Stand up!"
And the man jumped to his feet and started walking.
ACTS 14:9–10

I want the kind of faith Paul saw in this crippled man—the faith to be healed! Your servant Paul's faith, coming into agreement with the faith of this man, resulted in a mighty healing miracle. Lord, help me to stand up and walk in faith, not fear. Lead me to praying people who will agree with my faith to be healed, people who trust in Your promises! Lord, let my faith be obvious to those around me so I am able to testify to Your faithfulness.

Yes and Amen!

For all of God's promises have been fulfilled in Christ with
a resounding "Yes!" And through Christ, our "Amen"
(which means "Yes") ascends to God for his glory.
2 CORINTHIANS 1:20

Lord, thank You for fulfilling all Your promises through Christ, the Messiah! When You came in the flesh to live among Your people, You were the visible image of the invisible God. You were completely faithful to Your mission and Your ministry, giving up Your rights as God and suffering a cruel death on the cross so I can live! Now, You continue to faithfully intercede for me in the throne room. Thank You, Lord, that I can expect You to fulfill all Your promises with a resounding "Yes" and "Amen!"

Faithful Promises

He will cover you with his feathers. He will shelter you with his wings. His faithful promises are your armor and protection.
Psalm 91:4

No matter how serious my situation becomes and no matter how desperate I am for a breakthrough, You, Lord, are faithful. I trade all my fears for faith in You. Thank You for covering me with Your feathers and sheltering me with Your wings! Your faithful promises are the very armor that protects me from this cancer. Help me to find rest in You. Help me to fully trust in Your protection. Your faithfulness will keep me safe.

⁓

Faithful Regardless

True, some of them were unfaithful; but just because they were unfaithful, does that mean God will be unfaithful?
Romans 3:3

It doesn't matter what the world may say about this cancer diagnosis. Ultimately, it doesn't even matter what the doctor says. If You say one thing, and the entire world says another, Your word is always true. You have the final authority. You speak truth and cannot lie. You never change, and Your word never changes. Lord, help me to trust Your message of hope over the world's message of hopelessness. Help me to believe Your truth even if nobody else believes it. Lord, thank You that You are always faithful. No matter what happens, my future is always secure in Your hands.

Promise Keeper

God will do this, for he is faithful to do what he says,
and he has invited you into partnership
with his Son, Jesus Christ our Lord.
1 Corinthians 1:9

Lord, that I am in an eternal partnership with the Creator of the universe is beyond human comprehension! Regardless of what is happening around me, help me to stand in faithfulness that You always do what You say. Lord, help me to pray expectantly, believing I will receive. Help me to walk through the tension when my circumstances seem to contradict Your promises, so that nothing shakes my faith in what I know to be true. You are the ultimate Promise Keeper. Even when I don't understand, I can trust You are faithful to do what You say.

Chapter 15: His Peace

Not of This World

*"I am leaving you with a gift—peace of mind and heart.
And the peace I give is a gift the world cannot give.
So don't be troubled or afraid."*
JOHN 14:27

My child, I know how you worry. What is on the other side of this cancer? Will there be another side? What will the future bring? I feel your anxiety at each doctor appointment and through every treatment. I know the fear that paralyzes you as you wait for the results of every test. Your heart races, your chest tightens, and a sick feeling churns deep in the pit of your stomach as you anticipate the worst. You wonder if this nightmare will ever end. Will you ever have peace?

Beloved, you need not be troubled or afraid, for I have left you with a wonderful gift. My peace is your weapon against worry and fear. My peace is completely different from the world's peace. The world's peace is tied to circumstances. You feel peace when things go smoothly and upset when they don't. But My peace is eternal and forever. It is not found in positive thinking or a good lab report. My peace comes when you trust Me, regardless of what happens around you. It comes from knowing that I alone control your future. Right now, you can exchange all your fears for a peace of such magnitude you cannot begin to grasp its scope and power.

My child, the true battle to keep your peace is in your mind. Any thought or worry that comes into your mind that is contrary to My Word and My character did not come from Me; it comes from the greatest deceiver of all time, the devil, who is a liar and the father of lies (John 8:44). But child, I am the commander of this battle. With your permission, I can destroy every lie that would keep your thoughts from agreeing with Mine (2 Corinthians 10:5). Choose daily to let Me control your mind and you *will* find My peace (Romans 8:6).

To keep My peace, you must turn all your worries, fears, and anxious thoughts into prayers of petition and thanks. Pray about every detail surrounding this cancer and every detail of your life. Tell Me what you need and thank Me for all I have done, and I promise you a peace far more wonderful than your human mind can understand (Philippians 4:6–7). Trust My perfect love to drive out your fear before it gains a foothold (1 John 4:18). Give Me all your worries because I care about what happens to you (1 Peter 5:7)!

Child, put on My armor so you can stand firm against your enemy (Ephesians 6:13–18)! Wear the helmet of salvation to protect your mind from doubting My saving work in your life (Ephesians 6:17). Put on the breastplate of righteousness to stay confident of your worthiness in Me (Ephesians 6:14). Let the belt of truth help you discern the enemy's lies and keep you focused on My healing promises. The shoes of peace give you the courage to walk boldly through this valley of cancer and proclaim the true peace found only in Me. Hold up the shield of faith to stop every fiery arrow the enemy throws at you (Ephesians 6:14–16). Finally, take the sword of the Spirit, My Word, and use it to counter the enemy's lies just like I did during My forty days in the wilderness (Ephesians 6:17; Matthew 4:1–11). There is no lie I haven't already defeated. Resist his lies daily with the truth of his defeat and the enemy must flee (James 4:7)!

Dear one, I am the Prince of Peace (Isaiah 9:6). The next time worry and fear threaten to steal your peace and tempt you to take your eyes off Me, simply say "I trust You, Lord" and fully expect Me to take care of it. My peace is not of this world.

PRAY

BLESSED WITH PEACE

The LORD gives his people strength.
The LORD blesses them with peace.
PSALM 29:11

Lord, help me always remember that the same power that raised You from the dead—the same power that controls creation itself—that same power is available to me today in my battle against this cancer. Help me always remember that my battle is really Your battle, Lord. Thank You for fighting for me. Even when I don't understand Your ways, I submit to Your plans and purposes for my life. Thank You for giving me Your strength to endure. Thank You for blessing me with Your peace through this journey.

PERFECT PEACE

You will keep in perfect peace all who trust in you,
all whose thoughts are fixed on you!
ISAIAH 26:3

Father, this cancer has turned my world upside down. Turmoil and uncertainty surround me daily. As someone who likes being in control, I have lost control! Thank You, Lord, that You have never once taken Your eyes off me. Because You are in control of my destiny, I can have perfect peace in You in spite of all the confusion. You are my stable rock in a world of shifting sand. In Your unchanging love and Your mighty power, I will not be shaken. Help me to fix my thoughts on You. Help me to trust You, Lord. Keep me in Your perfect peace.

Take Heart

"I have told you all this so that you may have peace in me.
Here on earth you will have many trials and sorrows.
But take heart, because I have overcome the world."
John 16:33

Lord, You defeated this cancer on the cross and took it with you to the grave. While the battle rages on around me and the enemy tries to convince me otherwise, I already know the victorious outcome. You already won the ultimate victory when You rose from the dead. Lord, thank You that I am never alone in the trials and sorrows I face on this earth. You have already overcome them all, including this cancer. Help me to claim Your peace throughout this journey. In the midst of all the uncertainty, help me remember I can be certain of You.

No Fear

Though a mighty army surrounds me, my heart will not be afraid.
Even if I am attacked, I will remain confident.
Psalm 27:3

This cancer feels like a mighty army surrounding me, Lord. With each new attack, the fear of this disease and my unknown future intensifies until it holds me captive. I feel stuck in a constant state of waiting—waiting for doctors, waiting for test results, waiting for this nightmare to end, and fearing it never will. But, Lord, You can set me free from my prison of fear. I'm sorry for coming in agreement with fear and allowing it to torment me. I give You my fear and trade it for Your peace. Fear, you no longer have any power over me! Lord, I choose to trust You instead. Thank You for setting me free. Thank You for the gift of Your peace. Though it may seem like this cancer has me surrounded, my heart will know no fear.

Victorious Right Hand

Don't be afraid, for I am with you. Don't be discouraged, for I am
your God. I will strengthen you and help you. I will hold
you up with my victorious right hand.
Isaiah 41:10

God, thank You for Your amazing promises! I never need to be afraid because You are with me and will never leave or forsake me. I never need to be discouraged because You alone are my God and You are fighting for me. When I feel weak and helpless, You will strengthen me and help me. When I begin to sink into the pit of despair, You pull me out and hold me up with Your victorious right hand. Lord, thank You for choosing me and loving me. In You, I am victorious over anything that comes against me.

Not from God

For God has not given us a spirit of fear and timidity,
but of power, love, and self-discipline.
2 Timothy 1:7

Lord, fear is not from You! Instead, You have given me power, love, and a sound mind. Help me not to be intimidated by this cancer, Lord. When I am tempted to fear, help me to remember You are stronger and more powerful than this cancer and everything that comes with it. Help me to walk boldly through this valley of cancer with You at my side, trusting in Your peace, Your power, and Your provision.

Cast Your Cares

Give all your worries and cares to God, for he cares about you. Stay alert! Watch out for your great enemy, the devil. He prowls around like a roaring lion, looking for someone to devour.
1 Peter 5:7–8

Forgive me, Father, when I carry the burden of this cancer and all my worries and concerns on my own shoulders. I'm sorry for not always admitting my own need and allowing others to help me! When I'm weak, helpless, and cut myself off from friends and family, I can be a target for the enemy's lies and attacks. Lord, I give You all my worries and cares. Help me keep my eyes on You and trust that You care about me. Give me the courage to allow others to come alongside me in this journey.

Beyond Human Understanding

Do not be anxious about anything, but in every situation, by prayer and petition, with thanksgiving, present your requests to God. And the peace of God, which transcends all understanding, will guard your hearts and your minds in Christ Jesus.
Philippians 4:6–7 niv

Lord, when my peace comes from my worldly circumstances, my life becomes an emotional roller coaster of ups and downs, good news and bad news, good days and bad days. Help me off this roller coaster! Help me turn every worry and every anxious thought into a prayer. Remind me to thank You for all my blessings and tell You exactly what I need so I can experience *Your* peace, not the temporary peace the world gives. Your peace comes from knowing You are with me through every difficult situation. My citizenship in Your kingdom is assured, my destiny is set, and I have victory in You, regardless of what the world says or thinks. Lord, guard my heart and mind against anxiety. I want off the roller coaster. I want to experience a supernatural peace that transcends all human understanding. I want Your peace. I want You.

Take Every Thought Captive

We demolish arguments and every pretension that sets itself up against the knowledge of God, and we take captive every thought to make it obedient to Christ.
2 Corinthians 10:5 NIV

As soon as I allow my mind to worry and entertain anxious thoughts and possibilities, I immediately lose my peace. Please protect me from any person or message that causes me to doubt Your truth and partner with fear, whether the Internet, a well-meaning friend or family member, or even a trusted doctor. Lord, I give You control of my thoughts and my mind. I surrender every thought or argument that is not from You, every worry, every lie, and every fear that blocks or opposes my knowledge of Your nature and Your promises. I trust You, Lord. Take every thought captive under Your authority.

He Will Flee

So humble yourselves before God. Resist the devil, and he will flee from you.
James 4:7

Lord, You have already won the battle against cancer. You finished it once and for all at Calvary. When You return, the devil and all he stands for will be eliminated forever. In the meantime, he is still here trying to torment me with his lies and distract me from my devotion to You and Your promise of victory. In the power of Your Spirit and in Your name, I refuse to submit to his lies and tricks. Get behind me! Jesus is my Lord and King!

Rest for Your Weary Soul

*Then Jesus said, "Come to me, all of you who are weary and carry heavy
burdens, and I will give you rest. Take my yoke upon you. Let me teach
you, because I am humble and gentle at heart, and you will
find rest for your souls. For my yoke is easy to bear,
and the burden I give you is light."*
Matthew 11:28–30

Father, often the burden of this cancer becomes so heavy I can't
carry it anymore. I'm weary, Lord. I'm tired of waiting rooms, doctors, treatments, and uncertainty. You promise there is light and life
on the other side of this dark valley, but sometimes I feel like I'll
never get there. The burden is too heavy, and I can't carry it anymore.
I need You, Lord. Help me to give this burden to You. I give You
all the worry, fear, pain, doubt, and uncertainty. I give You all the
drugs, treatments, side effects, and medical opinions. Most of all, I
give You the outcome. Lord, when I step into the light on the other
side, it will be by Your power alone. I come to You. My soul needs rest.

Trust in Him

*I pray that God, the source of hope, will fill you completely with joy
and peace because you trust in him. Then you will overflow
with confident hope through the power of the Holy Spirit.*
Romans 15:13

You are the source of all hope. I desperately want to be completely
filled with Your joy and peace! Please reveal any thoughts, doubts, or
false beliefs that would stand in the way of my trusting You. Replace
these lies with Your truth, Lord. Help me to focus on You and Your
promises, regardless of the circumstances around me. You are God,
and You are holy, regardless of cancer or anything else that might
come against me! Lord, let my confident hope in You overflow!
Thank You for hope today, hope for tomorrow, and hope for the
future.

LORD OF PEACE

*Now may the Lord of peace himself give you his peace at all times
and in every situation. The Lord be with you all.*
2 THESSALONIANS 3:16

Lord, You don't just give me Your peace. You *are* peace. When I
lose my peace, I've taken my eyes off You, focused on my problems
and the cares of the world, and stepped away from Your presence.
Forgive me, Lord! I know You never leave me or forsake me. You
are always with me. Please draw me back into fellowship with You!
Draw me back to that place of intimacy where I can rest in You and
hear Your still small voice. I want to live in this place, Lord! I want
to experience Your peace at *all* times and in *every* situation! Keep my
eyes firmly focused on You. You are the Lord of peace!

MORE LORD

*May God give you more and more grace and peace as you grow
in your knowledge of God and Jesus our Lord.*
2 PETER 1:2

Thank You for revealing the secret to having more peace—growing
in my knowledge of You! Through every trial on this earth, You
reveal more of Your character and more of Your love for me. When
this cancer takes me to the end of myself and my own power, You
reach out and take my hand, leading me to places of intimacy with
You I could never otherwise go. Lord, I want more! I want to know
You. Reveal Yourself to me through Your precious Word. Help me
stop and listen to Your voice when I pray. I want more of Your
grace and more of Your peace! Lord, I want more of You! I want
more because You are all I need. You are enough.

Chapter 16: His Righteousness

Through Heaven's Eyes

For he raised us from the dead along with Christ and seated us with him in the heavenly realms because we are united with Christ Jesus.
Ephesians 2:6

My child, you may have cancer, but this cancer is not your identity. When I look at you, I don't see a cancer patient. I don't see a victim. I see My precious and perfect child, a new creation, reconciled to Me by faith; redeemed, forgiven, and healed by My blood (Romans 5:1; Colossians 1:13–14). If you allow this cancer to become your identity, a dark cloud of doubt and uncertainty will threaten to rain on your future. But, child, you need not live under the shadow of this cancer. You wear My beautiful robe of righteousness, because I am righteousness (Isaiah 61:10; 2 Corinthians 5:21). I loved you first, called you out of darkness and into the light, and adopted you into My family (1 Peter 2:9; 1 Thessalonians 4:1). As a child of a King, you are a full heir to My estate, and your royal position is secure. I raised you up with Me and seated you in the heavenly realms. Everything that belongs to Me also belongs to you!

Beloved, remember, there is no condemnation in Me (Romans 8:1). You may know all your flaws and weaknesses, but I see you only as righteous and holy (Ephesians 4:24). I already died for every mistake you will ever make. You are a partaker of My divine nature and perfect in My eyes (2 Peter 1:3–4). You may be facing cancer, but I have already conquered cancer and death. You are already redeemed from the curse of sin, sickness, and poverty (Galatians 3:13). In Me, you live in victory as a citizen of heaven where no evil can touch you (Philippians 3:20; 1 John 5:18).

Dear one, let My righteousness define you. Your true identity comes from the one who created you and watched as you were woven together in the darkness of the womb (Psalm 139:14–15). It comes from the one who suffered a cruel death for your mistakes and the sins of the world (Romans 3:24–25). And it comes from the one within you who is greater than he who is of this world (1 John 4:4). You are My masterpiece, and I created you with a purpose (Ephesians 2:10). My plans for your life are far more wonderful than anything your limited human mind can imagine (Isaiah 55:8–9). You have unique gifts and a special calling on your life, and I have chosen and appointed you to bear fruit for My kingdom (John 15:16; 1 Corinthians 12:27).

My child, I will not let this cancer steal your destiny. Will you choose to walk every day in the knowledge of who you are and whose you are? You can agree with Me, and live every day in the healing and freedom I died for, regardless of what is happening around you, fully knowing you are saved, healed, and set free by My blood. Or you can agree with the enemy and live the old life I already redeemed you from. Child, you fight this battle from a place of victory, standing firm in My breastplate of righteousness (Ephesians 6:14). Through heaven's eyes, you are My perfect child resting safely and securely in My loving arms, with a destiny and purpose to fulfill for My glory. Through heaven's eyes, you are the child you were born to be.

PRAY

Righteous by Faith

*Therefore, since we have been made right in God's sight by faith,
we have peace with God because of what Jesus
Christ our Lord has done for us.*
Romans 5:1

Lord, I know that my peace is not based on feelings of calmness or tranquility. It comes from knowing that, because of the price You paid on the cross, no sin or sickness is standing in the way of my relationship with You. Thank You for the gift of faith that makes me righteous and complete in Your sight. Thank You for the gift of grace that helps me to grow into Your likeness as I face the problems of this world.

Chosen to Be Holy

*Even before he made the world, God loved us and chose us
in Christ to be holy and without fault in his eyes.*
Ephesians 1:4

You are the righteous and holy one, God. When You became human and faced the same challenges and emotions I face every day, You never sinned. I can hardly grasp that You loved me even before You made the world. You chose me to be like You, holy and without fault. When You look at me, you don't see my flaws and shortcomings. You see me through the lens of Jesus, who died to make me righteous. Show me what You see when you look at me, Lord. Help me to walk through this cancer every day knowing the truth of my identity, that I am Your chosen one, holy and without fault in Your eyes.

His Gift of Righteousness

For the sin of this one man, Adam, caused death to rule over many.
But even greater is God's wonderful grace and his gift of righteousness,
for all who receive it will live in triumph over sin and
death through this one man, Jesus Christ.
Romans 5:17

Lord, when You became my Savior, I traded the sinful nature I inherited from Adam for Your righteousness once and for all! Your righteousness triumphed over sin, sickness, and death. Lord, I receive Your wonderful grace and Your gift of righteousness! My life is secure in You, today and forever. Like You, and by Your power, I can reign over sin and the enemy's threats and ruthless attacks! Thank You, Lord! In You, I live in triumph over sin and death.

Righteous and Holy

Put on your new nature, created to be like God—
truly righteous and holy.
Ephesians 4:24

Help me put my old ways behind me, Father. My old nature is like old, dirty, worn clothing. Lord, I want to live as You created me to live! Change me from the inside out, Lord. Let Your righteousness manifest in my spirit, soul, and body. In Your power, I can be like You—truly righteous and holy. You are not calling me out on my mistakes and shortcomings, because You already took care of every mistake I will ever make. Thank You, Lord, for calling me up, to be who You created me to be!

His Wonderful Light

But you are not like that, for you are a chosen people. You are royal
priests, a holy nation, God's very own possession. As a result,
you can show others the goodness of God, for he called you
out of the darkness into his wonderful light.
1 Peter 2:9

Lord, thank You for making me a member of a royal priesthood! In the Old Testament, Your people had to communicate through a priest or intermediary. But Your death and resurrection made it possible for me to come directly to You and bring others with me! Lord, thank You that I can co-labor with You to advance Your kingdom here on earth. Thank You for calling me out of the darkness and into Your wonderful light. Lord, use me and this cancer to show others Your goodness. My worth and value are not based on my accomplishments, my successes, or even my health. I am Your very own possession. I am worthy in You alone.

Heirs of God's Glory

And since we are his children, we are his heirs. In fact,
together with Christ we are heirs of God's glory. But if we
are to share his glory, we must also share his suffering.
Romans 8:17

Thank You, heavenly Father, that I am an heir of Your glory, and a full heir to Your estate. As Your child, I have all the privileges and responsibilities of a child in Your family, and full access to all Your blessings, treasures, and gifts. Like all the heroes of faith before me, being Your child can sometimes come with a cost. Sometimes my family members, friends, and even some in the medical community may be skeptical of my commitment to You and Your Word. When I feel misunderstood, alone in my walk with You, or even persecuted for my beliefs, help me to love like You love. Help me to stand on Your truth without conforming to the ways of the world.

His Divine Nature

By his divine power, God has given us everything we need for living a godly
life. We have received all of this by coming to know him, the one who called
us to himself by means of his marvelous glory and excellence. And because of
his glory and excellence, he has given us great and precious promises.
These are the promises that enable you to share his divine nature
and escape the world's corruption caused by human desires.
2 PETER 1:3–4

Lord, the power to grow in Christ's likeness is not my own. It comes from Your Spirit within me, the one who called me by means of Your marvelous glory and excellence! Thank You that You made me a participant in Your divine nature, and You have given me everything I need for living a godly and faith-filled life. Thank You that through Your own glory and excellence, You have given me such great and precious promises. In You, I have the power to escape the world's corruption.

⌒

Complete in Christ

So you also are complete through your union with Christ,
who is the head over every ruler and authority.
COLOSSIANS 2:10

God, You alone are the head over every other ruler and authority. Thank You for providing the doctors who care for me. While I am richly blessed by their human knowledge and wisdom, I know You are the final authority. You alone hold the keys to life, because You are life itself. You are my only true source of knowledge and power. However it comes, all healing comes from Your hands. Lord, during the course of my treatment, protect me from any spiritual method or resource that claims to heal or add to my well-being that is not from You. Forgive me if I have been involved in any false religions, cults, or unbiblical philosophies in my quest for healing and wholeness. Thank You for Your righteousness, Lord. You alone complete me.

HELD SECURELY

We know that God's children do not make a practice of sinning,
for God's Son holds them securely, and the evil one cannot touch them.
1 JOHN 5:18

Even though Your righteousness has made me holy and I have turned my heart toward You, I can still fall into disobedience. Sometimes, I'm not even aware of my involvement in something sinful. But even then, I can admit my mistakes to You, and Your blood cleanses me from all unrighteousness and restores our relationship. Lord, forgive my disobedience. Give me Your strength to resist temptation. In You, I am free at last from the grip of the Evil One. In Your power, I am under no obligation to follow my fleshly desires or the behaviors and customs of the world. Lord, help me to be obedient to Your plans and purposes for my life. Thank You for Your grace and power to overcome!

ROBE OF RIGHTEOUSNESS

I am overwhelmed with joy in the LORD my God! For he has
dressed me with the clothing of salvation and draped me in
a robe of righteousness. I am like a bridegroom dressed for
his wedding or a bride with her jewels.
ISAIAH 61:10

You have dressed me in the clothing of salvation and draped me in a robe of righteousness. Nothing else matters, Lord. It doesn't matter what others think of me and my future. It doesn't matter what this cancer threatens to do to me. For I am like a bridegroom dressed for his wedding or a bride with her jewels! I am Yours, Lord. I am pure and spotless in Your sight. I am healed and whole. I am complete in You. I am overwhelmed with joy in the Lord my God!

He Is Greater

You are of God, little children, and have overcome them,
because He who is in you is greater than he who is in the world.
1 John 4:4 nkjv

Lord, it is so easy to let this cancer define me. All the doctor visits, treatments, and tests—I want it to be over! Lord, I just want my life back. But even as I wait, I know You are far greater than any problem I will ever face in this world. You are stronger than this cancer, and You have already conquered it. Lord, thank You that Your victorious spirit lives in my heart! When I feel overwhelmed and impatient, help me focus on the one who is greater than he who is in the world. Help me, Lord. Enlarge my faith until it overcomes this disease! Yes, Lord. You are greater.

Overwhelming Victory

No, despite all these things, overwhelming victory
is ours through Christ, who loved us.
Romans 8:37

Forgive me when I doubt Your sound victory over this disease, Lord! Your death proved Your love for me, and Your resurrection proved Your power over sin and death. Thank You that nothing can ever separate me from Your love. Thank You for never abandoning me. Lord, my future is secure in You, regardless of my circumstances. Through You, overwhelming victory is mine despite my current troubles, or whether I am persecuted, in danger, or even threatened with death. Yes, Lord. Your love defeated this cancer once and for all.

On Your Side

What shall we say about such wonderful things as these?
If God is for us, who can ever be against us?
ROMANS 8:31

Even though I know You made me righteous, there are still times I feel unworthy of Your love. Forgive me, Lord, when I doubt I am "good enough" to receive from You. Forgive me for believing Your blood isn't enough to save me and make me perfect in Your sight! Thank You that Your grace makes me worthy to receive Your gift of healing and restoration! Lord, You gave Your life for me! You made me worthy to receive all the blessings of Your kingdom. Thank You for being on my side of this battle! If You are for me, how can this cancer defeat me?

No Shadow of Shame

Those who look to him are radiant;
their faces are never covered with shame.
PSALM 34:5 NIV

Thank You for reminding me of who I am and whose I am! When the whole human race was on death row, You set us free and declared us not guilty! There is no condemnation in You, Lord. You separated my brokenness from me and never remembered it again. Thank You that my past doesn't define me. I don't need to be stuck in my past because You have totally forgotten it! Any shame I still carry, I give it to You now. Lord, this cancer is not my identity, and I am not a victim. I look to You, a child of Yours, my face radiant from the glow of Your presence. Thank You, Lord! You are my only hope. In You, no shadow of shame will ever darken my face.

Chapter 17: His Sovereignty

All Things Work Together

And we know that God causes everything to work together for the good of those who love God and are called according to his purpose for them.
ROMANS 8:28

My child, I am sovereign. All things are under My rule and control. I have the right, authority, and power to govern all that happens in accordance with My plans and purposes. You may wonder if I am in control. And if I am a good and loving God, how could this cancer happen to you? It is because I loved My creation so much, I allowed free choice. As a result, you live in a broken world where sin and sickness came into the paradise I created for you. Brokenness can result from the sin of others, from your own shortcomings, or from an attack from the evil one. My ways are higher than your ways, so often, you may never know (Isaiah 55:9). Regardless of why, I promise to cause everything to work together for your good as you walk according to My purpose for you.

One thing you must know is that I am sovereign over your healing. I have many ways to heal, and My methods and timing are not always predictable. It's never up to you to decide how or when, but however healing comes, I control it all. I am the one who heals all your diseases (Exodus 15:26; Psalm 103:3). I can heal by physicians, surgeons, climate, renewed mind-sets, common sense, or even a direct touch from My Spirit.

I give you wise physicians that prescribe medications to destroy mutated cells, kill harmful organisms, and regulate body systems. My surgeons have the ability to remove unwanted tissues and repair defective organs. I can use sunny, dry weather to bring health to your stiff and crippled bones. I provide counselors and ministers of inner healing to help you heal from wrong mind-sets and the wounds of your past that can impact your physical health. When you forgive and release bitterness, I can rewire your old toxic thought processes and cause your body, soul, and spirit to be healed and restored. I also gave you common sense and a sound mind to make good choices. I established natural laws for health and wellness, and your health can improve greatly when you avoid harmful addictive behaviors and take good care of your body. Sometimes I will bypass these natural methods and heal through a direct touch from My Spirit. However you receive healing, there is no second-class outcome. Being healed miraculously is not "more spiritual" than being healed medically. Healing by any method is a blessing from My hands.

My child, you are exclusively dependent on Me for your breath and sustenance. Never let your trust move subtly to the doctors, the drugs, or your own healthy choices instead of Me, for I am sovereign over all. I am the one power without limits that can never be destroyed. I will walk you through the tension when your circumstances don't appear to line up with My promises. And here is My greatest promise of all—I always heal eternally. You live in a mortal world where physical death is a reality for everyone. But in Me, you have the promise of immortality. Surrender yourself to My sovereignty. Surrender to My plans and purposes for your life. I am the Healer, and I make all things work together for good according to My plans and purposes.

PRAY

As He Wishes

Our God is in the heavens, and he does as he wishes.
PSALM 115:3

Lord, forgive me when I question Your sovereignty, authority, and justice because I don't always understand Your plans and purposes. Thank You that everything good in my life comes from Your hands. You do not change like the world changes. You are my one constant at a time of confusion and uncertainty. Your power is without limits. Lord, You are in the heavens, and You do as you wish. I only need to know You are a good and faithful God. I can always trust You to do what is best for me.

Lord Over All

He prayed, "O LORD, God of our ancestors, you alone are the God who is in heaven. You are ruler of all the kingdoms of the earth. You are powerful and mighty; no one can stand against you!"
2 CHRONICLES 20:6

God, You alone are ruler of all the kingdoms of the earth. How great is Your power, glory, and majesty! I seek Your favor, Lord. I belong to You. You created me, watch over me, and You are sovereign over all my circumstances. I am completely dependent on You alone. I praise You, Lord, and I take comfort in all of Your promises! You are powerful and mighty, and this cancer can't stand against You. Help me to trust the only one who can save me. You are Lord over all.

Intended for Good

You intended to harm me, but God intended it all for good.
He brought me to this position so I could save the lives of many people.
Genesis 50:20

Lord, You brought good from the sins of Joseph's brothers. When their jealousy drove them to sell him into slavery, he spent thirteen years in captivity. Through all of his trying experiences, You showed how you can bring good out of evil for those who trust in You. Joseph became ruler of Egypt and saved his brothers, their families, and the entire nation of Israel from famine and starvation. You can do the same for me, Lord. You can take this cancer that the enemy intended to harm me and use it all for good. I trust You, Lord! Use this cancer to bring about Your purposes! All for Your glory!

His Purposes Prevail

You can make many plans, but the LORD's purpose will prevail.
Proverbs 19:21

Lord, You know this cancer was not in my life plan! Thank You that Your purposes will prevail, regardless of my plans. I'm sorry when I've held on too tightly to my earthly plans and schedules. Forgive me when I've been resistant to what You are showing me through this unexpected journey. Help me to know You, Lord. I want my plans to align with Yours. Your plans for my life are perfect, and Your purposes will always prevail.

By My Spirit

Then he said to me, "This is what the LORD says to Zerubbabel:
It is not by force nor by strength, but by my Spirit,
says the LORD of Heaven's Armies."
ZECHARIAH 4:6

Surviving this cancer is not dependent on how tough I am, the expertise of my doctors, or the power of the drugs they give me. This battle is fought, not by force or strength, but by Your Spirit alone. I'm sorry when I've taken my eyes off You and put all my trust in the world's weapons and my own strength. Thank You for being on my side of this battle, Lord. You are the commander of this army. Help me to trust in Your strength and power.

Wisdom to the Wise

And He changes the times and the seasons; He removes kings
and raises up kings; He gives wisdom to the wise and
knowledge to those who have understanding.
DANIEL 2:21 NKJV

God, You change the times and the seasons and govern the world according to Your plans and Your purposes. Thank You for giving wisdom to the wise and knowledge to those who have understanding. Sovereign Lord, if You created the universe and control all of nature and the world's events, You hold the keys to conquering this scourge of cancer. Please give the scientists, researchers, and doctors eyes to see and ears to hear—more wisdom, more knowledge, and more revelation! Thank You, Lord, for the dedicated healthcare professionals who walk alongside me through this journey.

In His Hands

And yet, O Lord, you are our Father. We are the clay,
and you are the potter. We all are formed by your hand.
Isaiah 64:8

Sovereign Lord, I have no right to demand anything from You. You are the Creator who controls all creation. I am the clay, and You are the potter who formed me in Your hands. My next breath—my very existence—depends on You alone. I humble myself before You, Lord. Who am I to question You? I don't need to know why, Lord. I only need to know You. I surrender my life to Your plans and purposes.

According to His Plan

Furthermore, because we are united with Christ, we have received
an inheritance from God, for he chose us in advance, and he makes
everything work out according to his plan.
Ephesians 1:11

Thank You, Father, that I am united with You and have a rich inheritance as a child of God. You chose me to be Your child before I was even born. In the midst of this cancer, I rest in the truth that You are my Lord, You love me, and You control all things. Your purpose in my life cannot be thwarted, no matter what the enemy might do. Thank You, Lord, for making everything work out according to Your plan.

Supreme over All

Now he is far above any ruler or authority or power or leader or anything else—not only in this world but also in the world to come.
EPHESIANS 1:21

Lord, You have the ultimate authority over the powers of this world and the world to come. You are the Messiah, the anointed one who came to save the world, not condemn it. Thank You that I have no need to fear the turmoil surrounding me, this cancer that threatens my future, or even death itself. You are far above all of it and already won the final victory. Your covenant with me has been signed and sealed by Your blood. My life on earth is merely a dot on an infinite line that extends from the past and into the future. I belong to You forever, Lord! I praise You! You are supreme over all.

God Alone

Remember the things I have done in the past. For I alone am God! I am God, and there is none like me. Only I can tell you the future before it even happens. Everything I plan will come to pass, for I do whatever I wish.
ISAIAH 46:9–10

Sometimes I waver between trusting in Your power and the worldly methods You created for healing and restoration. Forgive me when my hope shifts away from You to the doctors; the next treatment; and the things I can do, see, and experience. Forgive me when I pursue comfort, peace, and healing apart from You! Help me to rest in Your strength and power until nothing shakes my confidence in You. You know everything about me, and You know what my future will bring. Your purpose has always been to carry out Your good plans. Lord, You alone are God. There is none like You. You are my healer. You are my hope. You alone.

Recorded in Your Book

*You saw me before I was born. Every day of my life was recorded
in your book. Every moment was laid out
before a single day had passed.*
PSALM 139:16

Lord, how amazing to know that You saw me before I was born!
You recorded every day of my life in Your book, and laid out every
moment before a single day had passed! While this cancer was not
from You, it didn't take You by surprise. You already had a battle
plan to fight for me. You knew how You would use what the enemy
intended for evil for Your glory and purposes. What a comfort to
know You have never taken Your eyes off me from the very beginning. My heart overflows with gratitude!

Power to Please

*For God is working in you,
giving you the desire and the power to do what pleases him.*
PHILIPPIANS 2:13

Thank You, Lord, for not leaving me to my own resources through
this day-to-day struggle to obey You and live according to Your
plans! Your Spirit lives inside me and comes alongside me to give
me strength. But Lord, my life is transformed only when I submit to
Your control and leadership. Only then can I do what pleases You.
Lord, help me want to obey. Give me the desire and the power to do
what pleases You!

His Masterpiece

For we are God's masterpiece. He has created us anew in Christ Jesus,
so we can do the good things he planned for us long ago.
Ephesians 2:10

Sometimes Your words take my breath away. Thank You that I am Your masterpiece, a perfect work created in Your image! Forgive me when I have treated this masterpiece You have created with disrespect and viewed it as inferior work! Long ago, before I ever knew You, You planned all the good things I would do for Your glory. Help me, Lord. Help me to live like the masterpiece You created, the masterpiece You see when You look at me through the eyes of Christ Jesus.

Nothing Too Hard

"I am the Lord, the God of all the peoples of the world.
Is anything too hard for me?"
Jeremiah 32:27

Lord, I know this cancer doesn't intimidate You. You are stronger, Your power is greater, and You already defeated it. Forgive me when I doubt Your ability to do the impossible. You are the God of all the peoples of the world. You performed impossible feats and many signs and wonders through the heroes of the Bible. You healed the sick then, and You still heal today. Thank You for being my God, Lord. Nothing is too hard for You.

Chapter 18: His Timing

Delays Are Not Denials

Consider it pure joy, my brothers and sisters, whenever you face trials of many kinds, because you know that the testing of your faith produces perseverance. Let perseverance finish its work so that you may be mature and complete, not lacking anything.
JAMES 1:2–4 NIV

My child, I know you feel you are on a never-ending journey. Discouragement threatens to consume you, mentally, physically, and spiritually. Please don't lose hope when weariness begins to take its toll. Don't give up when your breakthrough tarries and time stands still. Please don't stop trusting Me when I don't answer your prayers in the way you expect or according to your schedule. Child, I am always with you. I will never leave you or forsake you (Hebrews 13:5). My timing is always perfect. Let perseverance finish its work in you so you may grow into the child I created you to be.

Persevere even when it feels as though I am not listening or I am ignoring your prayers. Persevere like the woman who had a dispute with an enemy and repeatedly took her request for justice to the judge who kept ignoring her. This judge neither feared Me nor cared about people, but he finally gave her justice because her persistence wore him out. If this unjust judge rendered a just decision, I will surely give justice to My chosen ones who cry out to Me day and night (Luke 18:1–8)! Child, don't pray a few times and give up because the answers didn't come as you expected. Even this evil judge relented. How much more will I, your loving Father, respond to your needs? Perseverance is an expression of your faith in Me. Never give up, even when the answers come slowly (Habakkuk 3:2). Trust Me, for I am the God of your breakthrough (1 Chronicles 14:11).

Dear one, there is much you can do when breakthrough tarries. Surround yourself with believing friends who will pray for you, encourage you, and lift you up. When you can't pray, take comfort in knowing that My Spirit prays for you with groaning that cannot be expressed in words in harmony with My own will (Romans 8:26–27). Worship Me, even when you least feel like it, for some have received their breakthrough by worshipping Me in the most desperate of circumstances (Acts 16:26)! Keep your requests continually before Me, and remind Me of My promises to meet your needs (Philippians 4:19). Yes beloved, pray without ceasing and give thanks in all circumstances (1 Thessalonians 5:16–18; Philippians 4:6–7). Take your mind off yourself by blessing others in their troubles with the same comfort I have given you (2 Corinthians 1:4). If you are struggling with unforgiveness, release your bitterness and forgive those who offended you, just as I have forgiven you (Colossians 3:12–13). Finally, stop striving and fighting on your own power. When you humble yourself before Me, I promise to lift you up (James 4:10).

In this place of waiting, let perseverance finish its perfect work. My power works best when you have finally reached the end of yourself (2 Corinthians 12:9). Take My hand and let Me lead you to places you have never known, where there is supernatural joy in the midst of the unthinkable. Beloved, knowing Me is much better than the healing you so desperately desire. While you wait, you are becoming mature and complete, not lacking anything. Child, My timing is perfect. Delays are *not* denials.

PRAY

WAIT FOR IT

For the vision is yet for an appointed time; but at the end it will speak, and it will not lie. Though it tarries, wait for it; because it will surely come, it will not tarry.

HABAKKUK 2:3 NKJV

Lord, this cancer consumes me. It takes up my time, dominates my thoughts, and threatens my future. I am waiting for Your response, Lord! I am waiting for Your appointed time! I know You hate this cancer just as much as I do. Help me to wait patiently. Help me to trust my breakthrough will surely come, even when I don't understand Your delays. Yes, Lord, it will come in Your timing, not mine. It will not tarry.

COME CLOSE

Come close to God, and God will come close to you. Wash your hands, you sinners; purify your hearts, for your loyalty is divided between God and the world.

JAMES 4:8

Lord, the waiting frustrates me. Forgive me when I push You away when things don't go as I hoped or planned. Once again, I humble myself before You and turn this cancer over to You and Your authority. Help me to resist the enemy's lies that You don't care, it's too late, or I've run out of options. Forgive me for doubting Your love and believing my situation is impossible for You. I'm sorry when I've put all my hope in the doctors, their treatments, and the world's methods instead of You. Purify my heart, Lord. I bow down before You. Only You can lift me up. Draw me close.

The Lord Who Breaks Through

So they went up to Baal Perazim, and David defeated them there. Then David said, "God has broken through my enemies by my hand like a breakthrough of water." Therefore they called the name of that place Baal Perazim.
1 Chronicles 14:11 NKJV

You called Your servant David a "man after Your own heart." He always turned to You before each battle and asked for guidance and protection. When You told him You would give him victory, he and his army defeated the Philistines and David named the place *Baal Perazim*, which means "The Lord Who Breaks Through." Lord, I need Your guidance and protection in each battle against this cancer. Break through this enemy, Lord! Let this cancer be my Baal Perazim.

Wait Patiently

Wait patiently for the LORD. Be brave and courageous. Yes, wait patiently for the LORD.
Psalm 27:14

Even though You anointed King David as king of Israel at age sixteen, he didn't actually become king until fourteen years later. During this time of waiting, while he was hiding in caves and running for his life from a jealous King Saul, You were preparing him for Your call on his life. He could have given up countless times, but he learned to wait patiently for Your plans to unfold. Lord, waiting on You isn't easy! I often wonder if You hear my cries or truly understand the urgency of my needs. Forgive me, Lord, for believing You have forgotten me or You are not being fair to me. Use this time of waiting to prepare me for Your purposes and to teach me Your ways. Lord, You are worth waiting for! Help me be brave and courageous. Thank You for revealing Yourself to me in this place of waiting.

Good to Those Who Wait

The LORD is good to those who wait for Him,
to the soul who seeks Him.
LAMENTATIONS 3:25 NKJV

Lord, no amount of human activity can speed up Your good plans and purposes for my life. All You want me to do in this time of waiting is to keep seeking after You. Please give me the strength and patience to keep waiting for You to act. Help me to trust You in the silence and resist stepping out ahead of You. Lord, I seek You with all my heart. Thank You for being so good to me!

Wings Like Eagles

Even the youths shall faint and be weary, and the young men shall
utterly fall, but those who wait on the LORD shall renew their strength;
they shall mount up with wings like eagles, they shall run
and not be weary, they shall walk and not faint.
ISAIAH 40:30–31 NKJV

When life crushes in, Father, even the strong and young grow weary. Thank You that Your power and strength will never fail me. You are always there to help me when I am so physically and emotionally fatigued, I can't make it through another day. Lord, help me to wait with patient expectation that You will fulfill Your promises. Renew my strength so I can mount up with wings like eagles and live high above this cancer!

CONFIDENT HOPE

Rejoice in our confident hope.
Be patient in trouble, and keep on praying.
ROMANS 12:12

You are a good God and have great plans for my future. Please give me patience when my troubles overwhelm me and I am tempted to give in to hopelessness. Let these times especially be a reminder for me to keep on praying, to keep my requests continually before You. Lord, give me the persistence of that woman who repeatedly took her request for justice before the judge until he finally relented. I submit to Your timing, Lord. Help me to persevere in faith. I rejoice in my confident hope in You!

CROWN OF LIFE

God blesses those who patiently endure testing and temptation.
Afterward they will receive the crown of life that God
has promised to those who love him.
JAMES 1:12

Lord, You have promised the crown of life for those who patiently endure testing and temptation. Your crown is not the glory and honor that is valued here on earth, but the crown of eternal life that lasts forever. Lord, help me to always praise You in the midst of this storm. Help me to remember that, whatever happens here, the best is yet to come. Forgive me when I doubt Your faithful promises. I look forward to my eternal blessing, the crown of faith for all who know You and love You.

A Hope without Disappointment

We can rejoice, too, when we run into problems and trials, for we know
that they help us develop endurance. And endurance develops strength
of character, and character strengthens our confident hope of salvation.
And this hope will not lead to disappointment. For we know how
dearly God loves us, because he has given us the
Holy Spirit to fill our hearts with his love.
ROMANS 5:3–5

Father, to be honest, I don't feel like rejoicing when I run into problems and trials. You call me to rejoice, not because I should enjoy suffering or deny this cancer and its impact. You want me to rejoice because my trials can help me to grow in my relationship with You. Lord, use this cancer to develop my endurance. Endurance will strengthen my character, which in turn, deepens my confident hope for the future. Thank You for the promise that this hope will not lead to disappointment!

Strength to Endure

We also pray that you will be strengthened with all his glorious power so
you will have all the endurance and patience you need. May you be filled
with joy, always thanking the Father. He has enabled you to share in
the inheritance that belongs to his people, who live in the light.
COLOSSIANS 1:11–12

Yes, Lord, I pray that You will strengthen me with all Your glorious power so I will have all the endurance and patience I need! Thank You that I carry Your presence with me today, tomorrow, and into the future. When people expect me to be a sad and sullen cancer patient, may Your presence radiate such an irresistible joy that they are drawn to Your light! Give me opportunities to give the reason for my hope and tell them of the inheritance they can have in You. Thank You, Lord, for the strength to endure!

Running the Race

Therefore, since we are surrounded by such a huge crowd of witnesses to the life of faith, let us strip off every weight that slows us down, especially the sin that so easily trips us up. And let us run with endurance the race God has set before us. We do this by keeping our eyes on Jesus, the champion who initiates and perfects our faith. Because of the joy awaiting him, he endured the cross, disregarding its shame. Now he is seated in the place of honor beside God's throne.
Hebrews 12:1–2

The faithfulness of the huge cloud of witnesses who have gone before me gives me great encouragement to run the race with endurance that You have set before me. It's comforting to know that I don't battle alone, and I am not the first one to battle. Other faithful ones have run the race and won! Lord, help me to keep my eyes firmly planted on You, the Author and Perfecter of my faith. Reveal anything that stands in the way of my relationship with You and causes me to focus instead on my circumstances. You are the champion, Lord. I run for You alone.

Great Reward

So do not throw away this confident trust in the Lord. Remember the great reward it brings you! Patient endurance is what you need now, so that you will continue to do God's will. Then you will receive all that he has promised.
Hebrews 10:35–36

Lord, help me when I am tempted to throw away my confident trust in You! There are days when I get so discouraged and weary. Thank You for bringing people into my path to encourage my faith when I need it most! You seem to know when a phone call, a card, or a visit is exactly what I need to remind me that You have not abandoned me. Lord, I need patient endurance so I can grow in my faith and my relationship with You. Walk me through this valley so I can receive Your great reward.

Be Still

"The Lord will fight for you; you need only to be still."
Exodus 14:14 niv

Before You parted the Red Sea, God, Your people were trapped with Pharaoh's army closing in. After all those years in captivity, their dream of freedom was dead. They could see no way out. But Your servant Moses encouraged them to be still and let You fight for them. And Lord, You did! They stood back and watched You do the impossible. I, too, have waited patiently. My hopes rise and fall, but today I see no way out. I have no fight left. I can't take another step. Fight for me, Lord! Show me Your power. Show me what only You can do. Help me be still.

Fight the Good Fight

I have fought the good fight, I have finished the race,
and I have remained faithful.
2 Timothy 4:7

Lord, there will come a day when every single believer will meet You face-to-face. In that moment, we will take our last breath on this earth and our first breath in Your glorious presence. I reflect back on all the trials and troubles I have faced in this life and I marvel at Your faithfulness. Lord, whatever comes my way in the future, please give me the patience to wait on Your timing. Give me the strength to endure. Give me the faith to trust in Your promises. On that day when I behold Your glory, I want to be able to look into Your eyes and say, "Yes, Lord. I have fought the good fight, I have finished the race, and I have remained faithful."

Chapter 19: His Presence

The Secret Place

If you make the LORD your refuge, if you make the Most High your shelter, no evil will conquer you; no plague will come near your home.
PSALM 91:9–10

My servant David knew the secret place of My presence. I anointed him king when King Saul deliberately disobeyed Me. After killing Goliath and impressing King Saul with his musical talent and military successes, Saul took him into his home and treated him as a son. But when he realized David would replace him, his insane jealousy drove him into a murderous rage. David fled for his life with Saul and his army in relentless pursuit. He hid in caves in enemy territory for many years before Saul died and I made him king of Judah. Through it all, David's soul found shelter beneath My wings and rest in My shadow. I kept him secretly hidden in My pavilion, and My presence became his refuge and place of safety (Psalm 91:1–4; 31:20).

Although I had a special relationship with David, most of My Old Testament people sought My presence in the holy of holies, a sacred place in the temple that only priests could access in their behalf. But child, I came to earth as a man to make the secret place of My presence accessible to you and all believers! Your long-awaited Messiah came to break the power of sin and death (Mark 1:15)! When I became your Savior, you became My temple, and My presence now lives your heart (1 Corinthians 6:19).

Even though you carry My presence within you, there is still disease and sickness in the world. I will return someday to completely free the world of all sin, sickness, and evil (Romans 8:19–23). Until then, I am with you. I will be your shelter and refuge in times of trouble (Psalm 9:9). My child, all humanity finds shelter in the shadow of My wings (Psalm 36:7)! You can hide in My presence until this violent storm is past (Psalm 57:1). Let Me be your towering rock of safety, your safe refuge, a fortress where your enemies cannot reach you. Come and live forever in My sanctuary (Psalm 61:2–4)! In My presence, you will find protection from harm, courage to face your fears, and rest for your soul. Beloved, I am your hiding place, and I will surround you with songs of victory (Psalm 32:7).

Yes, child, come up here! Your mind is consumed by your circumstances, but I have seated you with Me in the heavenly realms (Ephesians 2:6). I want you to leave the world and this cancer behind and dwell with Me. Come up here and I will show you hidden things that you do not know, the deeper things of My heart (Jeremiah 33:3). You may have to fight through the lies of the enemy and the darkness of your soul to reach Me here (Matthew 11:12). But if you let Me, I will take you to a place where you are no longer moved by your circumstances, a place where you see through the eyes of faith (Philippians 4:11–12). When I look at you, I don't see cancer. Through My eyes, you are you healed and whole, regardless of the battle raging around you. Child, let Me wrap you in My glory. Make Me your dwelling place and no evil will befall you; no plague will come near your dwelling. Meet Me in the secret place.

PRAY

Pleasures Evermore

You will show me the way of life, granting me the joy of your presence
and the pleasures of living with you forever.
Psalm 16:11

True joy is deeper than the happiness found in good news or pleasant circumstances. True joy is only found in Your presence. Thank You that I can have Your joy in the midst of the pain and suffering of a cancer diagnosis! Your presence within me makes it possible for me to find contentment every day, regardless of anything that comes against me. Lord, help me to focus on You alone and reflect on Your wonders. Give me the joy of Your presence and the pleasure of living with You forever!

Shelter for the Oppressed

The LORD is a shelter for the oppressed, a refuge in times of trouble.
Those who know your name trust in you, for you, O LORD,
do not abandon those who search for you.
Psalm 9:9–10

Lord, there are no words to express my gratitude to You for sheltering me in this time of oppression. The enemy may want to steal my destiny, but You are my refuge in this time of deep trouble. Trials and sorrows in this world are bound to come. Yes, even cancer might attempt to steal, kill, and destroy. But You will not forsake those who seek You. You are my shelter, and I am trusting You.

Songs of Victory

For you are my hiding place; you protect me from trouble.
You surround me with songs of victory.
Psalm 32:7

Thank You for the victory You have already won for me on the cross. In this battle against cancer, I fight from an offensive position not a defensive position. I fight from a place of victory, not defeat! Protect me from the lies of the enemy who would try to convince me otherwise! Lord, this is Your battle and Yours alone. You are my defender, my hiding place, and my protector. Help me to hear Your songs of victory even before the victory is evident in the natural realm!

One Thing

The one thing I ask of the Lord—the thing I seek most—is to live in the house of the Lord all the days of my life, delighting in the Lord's perfections and meditating in his Temple. For he will conceal me there when troubles come; he will hide me in his sanctuary. He will place me out of reach on a high rock.
Psalm 27:4–5

Lord, King David's greatest desire was to live in Your presence every day of his life. This is my desire, Lord. I want to delight in Your perfections and meditate on Your glory. Lord, You are so amazing! I am Your temple, and Your presence dwells within me. Please remove the distractions that keep me from connecting with You and keeping my focus on You alone. Holy Spirit, speak to my spirit! Conceal me in Your presence in the midst of my troubles. Hide me in Your sanctuary. Place me on a high rock, out of reach from the enemy's lies and strategies. All I want is You, Lord. When I am in Your presence, only one thing matters: You.

In His Shadow

Those who live in the shelter of the Most High will find rest in the shadow of the Almighty. This I declare about the LORD: He alone is my refuge, my place of safety; he is my God, and I trust him. For he will rescue you from every trap and protect you from deadly disease.
PSALM 91:1–3

Help me, Father, when fear tries to torment me and keep me from trusting You! My heart's desire is to live every day in Your shelter and rest in Your shadow. Again today, I trade all my fears for trust in You. I trust in Your protection, Lord! You will rescue me from every trap and protect me from this fatal plague. You are my shelter. You are my refuge. You are my place of safety. You are my God, and I am trusting You.

$\backsim$

A Single Day

A single day in your courts is better than a thousand anywhere else! I would rather be a gatekeeper in the house of my God than live the good life in the homes of the wicked.
PSALM 84:10

Thank You, Lord, for using what the enemy intended for harm for Your glory and purposes. Thank You for using this cancer as a pathway to Your presence and an opportunity to experience more of Your love, Your power, Your promises, and Your faithfulness. Lord, there are some places deep within me that You cannot reach until I truly understand my brokenness and the depth of my need. I am reaching that place, Lord. I am learning that a single day in the courts of Your presence is better than a thousand days anywhere else. The best life in this world will never measure up to the life I have in You!

Times of Refreshment

Then times of refreshment will come from the presence of the Lord,
and he will again send you Jesus, your appointed Messiah.
Acts 3:20

Lord, I need You! I need a touch from You, especially today. The darkness surrounds me, but You can break into my circumstances like the dawn breaks forth in the morning sky. Lord, please remove anything that stands in the way of my basking in Your glorious presence. Draw me close to Your heart and refresh my spirit!

A Place for You

"Don't let your hearts be troubled. Trust in God, and trust also in
me. There is more than enough room in my Father's home. If this were
not so, would I have told you that I am going to prepare a place for you?
When everything is ready, I will come and get you, so that you
will always be with me where I am."
John 14:1–3

My eternal life with You began the moment I first believed. Thank You that You have already cleared the way for me to reach my eternal home. You have made special preparations and will come and get me when everything is ready. But even on this side of heaven, I can taste my eternal home and enter Your place of sacred rest. Draw me into Your presence, Lord. Help me to trust You when my heart is troubled. Thank You that You are always with me, today, tomorrow, and forever.

COME

My heart has heard you say, "Come and talk with me."
And my heart responds, "LORD, I am coming."
PSALM 27:8

I can't hear You with my ears, Lord. I can't hear when You speak to my mind. It is my heart that truly hears You—Your Spirit speaking to my spirit. Lord, speak to my heart! Draw me into Your presence. My heart hears You say, "Child, come and talk with me." Lord, I am coming! I pour out my heart to You. You are the only one who truly hears my cries, understands my deepest longings, and meets my every need.

MOST HOLY

And so, dear brothers and sisters, we can boldly enter heaven's Most Holy
Place because of the blood of Jesus. By his death, Jesus opened a new
and life-giving way through the curtain into the Most Holy Place.
And since we have a great High Priest who rules over God's house,
let us go right into the presence of God with
sincere hearts fully trusting him.
HEBREWS 10:19–22

Lord, before You came to earth, only the High Priest could enter the most holy place in the temple, and only once a year on the Day of Atonement when he offered sacrifices for the nation's sins. But now, Lord, You are the High Priest! When You shed Your blood and died on the cross, the curtain tore in two giving all believers direct access to Your presence. Thank You, Lord, for opening a new and life-giving way into heaven's Most Holy Place! I come boldly into Your presence with a sincere and trusting heart.

Remain in Him

"Remain in me, and I will remain in you. For a branch cannot produce fruit if it is severed from the vine, and you cannot be fruitful unless you remain in me. Yes, I am the vine; you are the branches. Those who remain in me, and I in them, will produce much fruit. For apart from me you can do nothing."
John 15:4–5

Heavenly Father, You are always in relationship with me. I can never escape Your presence. I am the one who allows the world to distract me. As a result, I move in and out of fellowship with You. Forgive me, Lord! Help me to remain in You! You are the vine, and I am the branches. You are the source of all my nourishment! You plant Your promises in my heart and keep my faith alive. You are my very life, and apart from You, I can do nothing. Lord, help me to stay close.

Thirsty Soul

O God, you are my God; I earnestly search for you. My soul thirsts for you; my whole body longs for you in this parched and weary land where there is no water. I have seen you in your sanctuary and gazed upon your power and glory. Your unfailing love is better than life itself; how I praise you!
Psalm 63:1–3

Some days I feel like David when he was being pursued relentlessly by his enemies in the wilderness—days when my whole body longs for You in this parched and weary land where this cancer presses on! While I am surrounded by wonderful caregivers, there is a deep longing in my spirit that only You can satisfy. You are the only one who truly understands my hopes and fears. Only Your presence can truly satisfy. Lord, I have seen You in Your sanctuary and gazed upon Your power and glory! Only You can fill the God-sized hole in my heart. Only You can satisfy my thirsty soul. Yes, Lord! Your unfailing love is better than life itself!

Beneath the Shadow

Have mercy on me, O God, have mercy! I look to you for protection.
I will hide beneath the shadow of your wings until the danger passes by.
PSALM 57:1

Lord, have mercy, for I am overwhelmed! This attack on my body continues, even friendly fire from the treatments the doctors use to destroy this cancer. Lord, protect my body from the side effects of these drugs. Hold me close until this violent storm is past. You are my healer, Lord. You are my protector. I am hidden beneath the shadow of Your wings.

Forever in His Sanctuary

Lead me to the towering rock of safety, for you are my safe refuge,
a fortress where my enemies cannot reach me. Let me live forever
in your sanctuary, safe beneath the shelter of your wings!
PSALM 61:2–4

You are my only safe refuge, God. Even as this cancer pounds on the walls of Your fortress, it cannot reach me. You have already won this battle, Lord. In You, I am victorious. Lead me to the towering rock of safety where I will stand with You in triumph. I live forever in Your sanctuary—the sanctuary of Your presence!

Chapter 20: His Provision

Everything You Need

*Seek the Kingdom of God above all else, and live righteously,
and he will give you everything you need.*
MATTHEW 6:33

My child, there is no lack of supply in My heavenly storehouse. I have set you apart and delight in showering My lavish, unlimited love and provision on you. As a child of Mine, everything I have belongs to you (Galatians 4:7)! You are entitled to the same spiritual blessings I promised Abraham (Galatians 3:29)! Obey Me and walk in My ways, and I will bless you wherever you go and in whatever you do. I will conquer your enemies when they attack and scatter them in seven directions! You have direct access to Me, your Creator and Father, and I have claimed you as My very own. I will care for your every need at the proper time from My rich heavenly treasury. The entire world will stand in awe of the blessings I pour on you (Deuteronomy 28:1–13)!

Beloved, you know I provide, yet I see your doubts, worries, and what-ifs. *What if I have the wrong doctor? What if the surgeon didn't get all the cancer? What if I need chemo? Will I handle the side effects? What if the chemo doesn't work? What if the cancer has spread? What if something shows up on this test or the next? What if this backache is something more than a backache? What will the future bring?* Child, when these concerns dominate your thoughts, you have allowed fear to replace your faith. If I created the vast universe, I can meet your needs today (Matthew 6:25). Can all these worries add one moment to your life (Matthew 6:27)? Do you think I would ignore My very own child? I care for birds and flowers. Wouldn't I care more for you (Mathew 6:26; 28–30)? Yes, I already know all your needs. You must take this battle one day at a time (Matthew 6:34). You must choose to trust Me.

When these worries come, remember I taught you to turn them into prayers (Philippians 4:6). Tell Me what you need and wait for Me to provide. Never withhold your requests because you feel unworthy. You are My redeemed child, and there is no condemnation in Me (Romans 8:1). Never hold back because you don't want to get your hopes up, and fear I will disappoint. Tell Me what you need and expect to receive. Never tire of waiting. Some of My children stop asking altogether or rush out ahead of Me, taking matters into their own hands. But you, child, must never settle for less. You must wait for My very best.

Beloved, just as a mother knows how to care for her child, I know your needs and desires before you ask. You are a citizen of My kingdom and entitled to all My blessings. You can rest assured that when you ask, I answer. Sometimes the answer might be different than you expect. It might take longer than you would like for My provision to come. But it *will* come. My storehouse is full of packages and promises addressed just to you. Yes, child, I am *Jehova-Jireh*, the God who provides (Genesis 22:14). If you seek Me above everything you need from Me—when you hunger after Me as a child craves intimacy with an earthly mother above all else—I will surely give you everything you need and then some.

PRAY

THE LORD WILL PROVIDE

So Abraham called that place The LORD Will Provide.
And to this day it is said, "On the mountain of
the LORD it will be provided."
GENESIS 22:14 NIV

Lord, You provided a ram to be sacrificed in place of Abraham's son, but You did not spare Your own Son! In the same way, by Your death on the cross, You took my place. It humbles me to know this, Lord. I will never fully understand the sacrifice You made for me. I can never thank You enough for providing a way for me to be free! In this one selfless act, You saved my life from eternal destruction, healed my diseases, and delivered me from oppression and demonic strongholds. Lord, I want to receive everything You died for. I trust You will provide.

THE GOOD SHEPHERD

The LORD is my shepherd; I have all that I need.
PSALM 23:1

You are my Shepherd, and I am a sheep of Your flock. Like sheep depend on the shepherd for provision, guidance, and protection, I am fully dependent on You. Thank You for pursuing me when I wander away from You and get lost in this valley of cancer. Forgive me for putting my trust in others or my own abilities to get my needs met. Lord, help me to trust in You alone! I want to be Your obedient follower. Thank You for providing for me, guiding me, and protecting me. You are my Good Shepherd, and I have all that I need.

His Glorious Riches

*And this same God who takes care of me will supply all your needs
from his glorious riches, which have been given to us in Christ Jesus.*
Philippians 4:19

God, You promise to supply all my needs. Right now, I have many!
But I also have many blessings. Thank You, Lord! You already know
my needs before I ask. You know the desires of my heart. But You
also know what's best for me. Your plans and timing are perfect!
Lord, help my desires align with Yours. Pour out Your blessings from
Your storehouse of treasures. Deliver those packages and promises
addressed just to me! Thank You for taking such good care of me.

Far More Valuable

*"Look at the birds. They don't plant or harvest or store food in barns,
for your heavenly Father feeds them. And aren't you
far more valuable to him than they are?"*
Matthew 6:26

As Creator You always take care of Your creation. Whether plants,
birds, animals, or people, You feed them from the abundance of Your
own house. Lord, You created me, and yes, I am far more valuable to
you than the birds! Forgive me when I worry about what You promise to supply. Worry can impact my health, my relationships, and my
ability to function. Worst of all, it keeps me from trusting You. I give
You my worries, Lord. I choose to trust You instead.

Lacking Nothing

Fear the Lord, you his godly people, for those who fear him will have all they need. Even strong young lions sometimes go hungry, but those who trust in the Lord will lack no good thing.
Psalm 34:9–10

Lord, I praise You for Your goodness! Thank You for the promise that those who trust You will lack no good thing. When I call on You, You will always meet my needs, sometimes in unexpected ways. When Your provision doesn't come on my timetable or in the way I expect, help me remember that You always know what's best for me. Lord, use this time in the desert to increase my dependence on You. Drive my roots down deep into the soil of Your love. Yes, I need this cancer to be over. I need to be healed and restored. But Lord, I need You more. In You, I lack nothing.

Wait Expectantly

Listen to my voice in the morning, Lord. Each morning I bring my requests to you and wait expectantly.
Psalm 5:3

Help me hear Your voice in the early morning hours when my mind is clear and free of the day's problems. Each morning, I bring my requests to You, whether my schedule is filled with work, doctor visits, treatments, time with family and friends, or quiet time at home. Lord, I give You my day and wait expectantly for You to provide for every detail. I trust You, Lord.

All His

The earth is the LORD's, and everything in it.
The world and all its people belong to him.
PSALM 24:1

When I look at the stars in the moon-lit sky, hear the sounds of birds singing or children laughing, or watch the sun rise over the morning horizon, I marvel at the beauty of Your creation. It all belongs to You, Lord. I belong to You. This body belongs to You. You created me in Your image, and I am perfectly and wonderfully made. Lord, You promise to take care of Your creation. Please provide wise doctors and caregivers who will fight for me. Bring every diseased cell and organ in my body back into perfect alignment with the way You created me. Heal me, Lord. I am Yours.

Don't Worry about Tomorrow

"So don't worry about tomorrow, for tomorrow will bring
its own worries. Today's trouble is enough for today."
MATTHEW 6:34

I know I must make plans, God. You have given me a sound mind to make decisions and think ahead about my hopes and dreams, next steps, and schedules. But worrying about tomorrow is time wasted and shows a lack of trust in Your plans and provision. Forgive me, Lord! I'm sorry for allowing fear of the future to consume me and interfere with my intimacy with You today. I'm sorry for not trusting in Your guidance and provision. I give You my doubts and worries, Lord. I can never be certain about what tomorrow will bring. Thank You that I can always be certain of You.

Open Wide

For it was I, the LORD your God, who rescued you from the land of Egypt. Open your mouth wide, and I will fill it with good things.
PSALM 81:10

From the very beginning You have provided for Your people. You provided food and made clothes for the first man and woman in the Garden of Eden. You provided for Noah and his family when they needed to repopulate the earth after the flood. You provided food and protection for the Israelites when You rescued them from captivity and led them through the wilderness into the promised land of milk and honey. Lord, You *never* change. I have no reason to believe You will not provide everything I need through this wilderness journey. I open my mouth wide, Lord. Fill it with good things!

Provision in the Wilderness

*For forty years I led you through the wilderness,
yet your clothes and sandals did not wear out.*
DEUTERONOMY 29:5

Lord, for forty years, the Israelites wandered in the wilderness because they disobeyed You and refused to believe Your promises. All this time, they didn't notice how You cared for their daily needs. In forty years, even their clothes and sandals did not wear out! Lord, forgive me when I take for granted all the ways You care for me. I'm sorry when I take the credit or give credit to others for meeting my needs while ignoring Your hand in my provision. Lord, You are the true source of all my blessings. Thank You for supplying all my needs!

Your Promised Land

For this good news—that God has prepared this rest—has been announced to us just as it was to them. But it did them no good because they didn't share the faith of those who listened to God. For only we who believe can enter his rest.
Hebrews 4:2–3

Lord, the promise You made to the Israelites to deliver them into their promised land did them no good because they didn't believe You would provide for them. Only Joshua and Caleb believed. They, along with the next generation of Israelites, were able to enter Your place of rest. Lord, forgive me when I get discouraged and let my present difficulties today overshadow Your promise to provide for me. Only Your power can help me reach the end of this long and difficult wilderness journey. Lead me to the other side of this cancer, Lord. Help me bring this journey to completion. I don't want to linger at the border of my promised land, consumed by doubt, fear, or unbelief. Help me to step in faith into the fullness of Your promises!

Bread of Life

Jesus replied, "I am the bread of life. Whoever comes to me will never be hungry again. Whoever believes in me will never be thirsty."
John 6:35

You faithfully provided bread from heaven to sustain the Israelites through their wilderness journey. In the same way I need bread to satisfy my hunger and sustain my physical life, so must my spiritual hunger be satisfied. Lord, only You can satisfy my deepest needs and longings. Only You can nourish my soul and sustain me through this long and difficult journey. I come to You, Lord. In You, I will never be hungry or thirsty again. You are the bread of life.

So Much More

The lame man looked at them eagerly, expecting some money.
But Peter said, "I don't have any silver or gold for you. But I'll give
you what I have. In the name of Jesus Christ the
Nazarene, get up and walk!"
ACTS 3:5–6

Father, every day this lame beggar was put beside the Beautiful Gate so he could beg from those going into the temple. When he asked for money, Peter commanded in Your name that he get up and walk! He told Peter what he wanted, but You gave him what he really needed. You healed his feet and changed his life forever. In the same way, I ask You for everything I need to get through this cancer. I pray for peace, comfort, good doctors, no side effects, and a list of practical daily needs. But Lord, I believe You can give me so much more! Today, in Your precious name, I command this cancer to leave my body forever! I proclaim Your promises of healing and restoration!

⌒

Never Forsaken

Let your conduct be without covetousness; be content with such things
as you have. For He Himself has said, "I will never
leave you nor forsake you."
HEBREWS 13:5 NKJV

Forgive me, Lord, when I'm unsatisfied with all You have given me. Help me to be grateful for what I have instead of resenting what I am missing. It all comes from You, Lord. Help me to give back to Your kingdom out of my abundance instead of coveting and accumulating more. Lord, this world and all my possessions will pass away, but You will never leave me or forsake me! You are all I need, Lord. You are my provider, today and forever.

Chapter 21: His Glory

Enthroned on Your Praises

Yet you are holy, enthroned on the praises of Israel.
PSALM 22:3

Beloved, My heart responds to your praise and worship. King Jehoshaphat appointed praise singers to lead his army into battle when the army of Moab, Ammon, and Mount Seir attacked him. At the sound of the singers' voices, I set the enemy armies into confusion, and they fought against one another. Not a single one escaped, and all my people were spared (2 Chronicles 20:10–26). Nearly a thousand years later, Paul and Silas were thrown in a jail in Macedonia for preaching the Gospel. Even though they were severely beaten and placed in stocks in the dungeon to make sure they wouldn't escape, they sang hymns to Me as the other prisoners listened. I sent a massive earthquake that shook the prison to its foundations. All the doors flew open and the chains of every prisoner fell off, setting them all free (Acts 16:16–34)!

My child, this cancer may feel like a mighty army is marching against you, leaving you little chance of victory. You may feel imprisoned, bound in chains with no hope of escape. But praise can be your most powerful weapon when the enemy attacks. Expressing your sincere devotion for Me can push out the darkness from your circumstances. Dear one, I do not dwell in the darkness, and I am not found in this cancer. I dwell in your praises. My glory descends from the heavens when you praise and worship Me. It was so powerful in the praises of Jehoshaphat's army that it scattered the enemy and rendered them ineffective. It was so powerful in the worship of Paul and Silas that it shook the prison to its foundations and set the prisoners free. My glory sets the enemy running because he can't dwell in My presence (James 4:7). When you praise and worship Me, you are expressing your faith in Me and declaring that you fight from a place of victory (Romans 8:37).

Child, true worship is a matter of the heart. I am the God who held the oceans in My hand, who measured off the heavens with My fingers, and picks up the islands as if they had no weight at all (Isaiah 40:12, 15). I am the one who makes the clouds My chariot and rides upon the wings of the wind (Psalm 104:3), and who names the stars, brings them out one after another, and calls each by name to see that none are lost or strayed away (Isaiah 40:26). As I reveal My power and majesty to you through My Word and My presence, you are free to respond in reverence and adoration from a grateful and humble spirit. Child, open your heart to Me in worship, and I will soothe and refresh you in the depths of your spirit and inspire you to hunger for more.

Yes, beloved. Worship Me for who I am, in the midst of this trial. The enemy may have formed an army against you, but I have defeated this army. This current battle doesn't belong to you or your doctors. It belongs to Me. Send your praises ahead of each fight. Sing hymns of praise from your prison of cancer. Place your hope in My grace, My promises, and My power. Give honor and praise to the King of all kings. Watch the enemy scatter in confusion. Watch the chains fall off and the prison doors open. Child, I am enthroned in your praises. Lift your hands to the heavens and watch My glory fall.

PRAY

COME LET US WORSHIP

Come, let us sing to the LORD! Let us shout joyfully to the Rock of our salvation. Let us come to him with thanksgiving. Let us sing psalms of praise to him. . . . Come, let us worship and bow down. Let us kneel before the LORD our maker, for he is our God. We are the people he watches over, the flock under his care.
PSALM 95:1–2, 6–7

I admit there are days in the midst of this battle against cancer where worship is the furthest thing from my mind! God, on those days especially, remind me of the praise singers You sent to lead the Israelites into battle. I sing to You, Lord, and I send my praises ahead of each fight! I worship You, Lord! I bow down to the one who made me. I trust the one who watches over me with the battle plan against this cancer. I come to You with thanksgiving and shout with joy to the Rock of my salvation!

⌒

PRAISE THE LORD!

Praise the LORD! Praise God in his sanctuary; praise him in his mighty heaven! Praise him for his mighty works; praise his unequaled greatness! . . . Let everything that breathes sing praises to the LORD! Praise the LORD!
PSALM 150:1–2, 6

Lord, thank You for the gift of Psalms. Through every phase of this cancer journey, there is no human emotion I will ever experience that isn't felt by David and the other authors of this sacred book of poetry. The Psalms remind me that You are always with me, guiding, encouraging, and comforting me. The Psalms remind me to praise You! Lord, I praise You in your sanctuary, and I praise You in Your mighty heaven! I praise Your mighty works and unequaled greatness! Thank You for taking my hand and leading me through the highs and lows of this journey. My heart can offer You nothing else but praise and adoration.

With Thankful Hearts

Let the message about Christ, in all its richness, fill your lives.
Teach and counsel each other with all the wisdom he gives.
Sing psalms and hymns and spiritual songs to God with thankful hearts.
COLOSSIANS 3:16

I surrender all! I give You the concerns of this world, God, and all the unknowns that lie ahead. Let Your message of hope in all its richness fill my life and control my thoughts. I want to live by Your power, not my own. Please lead me to a community of believers who worship together, sing psalms and hymns and spiritual songs to You with thankful hearts! I want to share my life with like-minded people who will hold me accountable in my faith as we teach and counsel each other and grow in Your wisdom. Lord, my heart bursts with praise as You fill every need in my life!

Sacrifice of Praise

Therefore, let us offer through Jesus a continual sacrifice of
praise to God, proclaiming our allegiance to his name.
HEBREWS 13:15

When I think of the sacrifice You made for me, what can I possibly offer You in return? All I can give You is my continual sacrifice of praise. I pour myself out for You, Lord. I want to be all in. I give You all that I am and yield to all that You are. I praise You, Lord! I lift my hands to the heavens and proclaim my allegiance to Your name!

KING OF GLORY

*Who is the King of glory? The LORD, strong and mighty; the LORD,
invincible in battle. Open up, ancient gates! Open up, ancient doors,
and let the King of glory enter. Who is the King of glory?
The LORD of Heaven's Armies—he is the King of glory.*
PSALM 24:8–10

Lord, I am desperate for Your presence and power to come in and
finish this battle! You are the Lord Almighty, the promised Messiah who came to heal the sick, set the captives free, and release
the downtrodden from their oppressors. You are strong and mighty,
invincible against this cancer! Open up the gates and enter this battle! Heal me and set me free! You are the Lord of Heaven's Armies,
the King of Glory!

⌒

WORTHY OF PRAISE

*Sing a new song to the LORD! Let the whole earth sing to the LORD!
Sing to the LORD; praise his name. Each day proclaim the good news
that he saves. Publish his glorious deeds among the nations.
Tell everyone about the amazing things he does. Great is the
LORD! He is most worthy of praise!*
PSALM 96:1–4

I am overwhelmed by all the amazing things You have done for
me. As I reflect on Your power and majesty, my heart floods with
gratitude. Thank You for holding me close through this unexpected
storm! I can't help but proclaim this good news to the world! Lord,
You are the God who saves. All creation shouts Your praises! Give
me a new song to sing of Your glory and a new boldness to tell of
Your glorious deeds! Yes, Lord, You are great. You are worthy of
praise.

THE HEAVENS PROCLAIM HIS GLORY

*The heavens proclaim the glory of God. The skies display his
craftsmanship. Day after day they continue to speak;
night after night they make him known.*
PSALM 19:1–2

God, You reveal yourself in the vastness of the universe. The heavens
proclaim Your glory and the skies display Your craftsmanship. Your
power and splendor make me feel humbled by my own need. Day
after day, I am reminded of my brokenness and how desperately I
need a Savior. Yes, Lord, I feel so small and insignificant when I
gaze at the heavens, yet so significant that You would care for me!
You are the Creator of the universe—the one who crafted the sun to
shine by day, the moon to mark the seasons, and the stars to shine
by night— and yet I matter to You. Lord, I join with the heavens in
proclaiming Your glory!

SPIRIT AND TRUTH

*"But the time is coming—indeed it's here now—when true worshipers
will worship the Father in spirit and in truth. The Father is
looking for those who will worship him that way."*
JOHN 4:23

Your presence is not limited to time and space, Lord. Your Spirit
is present within me and everywhere! I can worship You anywhere
at any time, not just in church on Sunday. Lord, when I worship, I
don't want to just go through the motions. I want my worship to be
genuine and true, more than lifting up rote words and songs. I want
my knowledge of You to be more than intellectual understanding
of Your truth. Lord, thank You for your presence that dwells within
me! Your Spirit interacts with my soul; interprets Your Word for
me, making it come alive; and affirms who I am in You. Help me to
worship You in both spirit and truth!

As the Waters Cover the Sea

For the earth will be filled with the knowledge of the glory of the
Lord as the waters cover the sea.
HABAKKUK 2:14 NIV

Lord, You have blessed me with so much! I am surrounded by family and friends who care for me, a place to live, provision for my daily needs, and then some! I have access to good doctors, hospitals, clinics, and the latest drugs and treatments. All is good. Forgive me, Lord, when I allow the importance of these things to displace You. Lord, Your glory and majesty will outlive all my possessions. Lord, help me to pursue knowledge and understanding of You more than all the world's treasures! May the knowledge of Your glory fill the earth as the waters cover the sea!

Consuming Fire

Therefore, since we are receiving a kingdom that cannot be shaken,
let us be thankful, and so worship God acceptably with reverence
and awe, for our "God is a consuming fire."
HEBREWS 12:28–29 NIV

Eventually the world will crumble away and only Your kingdom will last. Thank You that I am part of Your everlasting kingdom! No matter what the future may bring—no matter the outcome of this cancer—my future is built on a solid foundation that cannot be destroyed. I do not put my confidence in the world's weapons that are here today and gone tomorrow and worldly knowledge that changes and advances with the times. Lord, I surrender all to You and Your kingdom. I worship You with reverence and awe that binds me to Your promises. I step into Your presence, Lord. Consume me with Your fire. In you, I am unshakable.

NOT TO US

*Not to us, O LORD, not to us, but to your name goes all the glory
for your unfailing love and faithfulness.*
PSALM 115:1

I have prayed with power for wise doctors and caregivers, drugs that
work, and for You to guide my surgeon's hands. In all this, Lord, You
have been faithful. Yet, let Your name alone be glorified. You alone
get the credit for my healing and restoration, not the medical realm,
family, friends, or even my pastor or my church. Not to us, but to
Your name goes all the praise and glory! Thank You, Lord.

LET YOUR LIGHT SHINE

*In the same way, let your light shine before others, that they may
see your good deeds and glorify your Father in heaven.*
MATTHEW 5:16 NIV

Father, I carry Your presence inside of me. When I live for You alone,
I can't help but to shine Your light before others. Lord, forgive me
when I hide my light out of fear of what others might think of me.
Please give me opportunities and boldness to share the reason for
my hope through my words and my actions. Regardless of my circumstances, help me to be a beacon of truth. Let my light shine for
Your glory.

Glory to Glory

But we all, with unveiled face, beholding as in a mirror the glory of the
Lord, are being transformed into the same image from glory
to glory, just as by the Spirit of the Lord.
2 Corinthians 3:18 nkjv

Only You, Lord, have the power to take a scourge like cancer and use it for Your glory and purposes. Thank You for the transforming power of Your Spirit within me! Throughout this journey, You have held me close to Your heart and revealed Your deepest secrets. You have walked with me through dark places I could never travel on my own. Lord, as I gaze into Your glory with the veil removed, I begin to catch a glimpse of Your reflection. Thank You for using this cancer to bring me closer to the person You see through your eyes, the person who is seated with You in the heavenly realms. Praise You, Lord! I am being changed into Your image from glory to glory.

All Glory to God

Now all glory to God, who is able, through his mighty power at work
within us, to accomplish infinitely more than we might ask or think.
Ephesians 3:20

Lord, I am standing on the threshold of tomorrow. I am a different person than I was when this journey began. In the beginning, I wanted to be healed. Today, I want You, the God who heals, the one who can accomplish infinitely more. I can't even imagine Your plans and purposes for me in this life and the life to come! But I know even my most impossible hopes and dreams for tomorrow are nothing for You to accomplish. Today, Lord, I declare Your glory! I have prayed these prayers with power and declared Your promises to the heavens. Now, seal in every declaration with Your precious blood. Through Your mighty power at work within me, You are able to accomplish infinitely more than I might ask or think! All the glory to You!

About the Author

Mary J. Nelson is an author, speaker, and pastor (non-staff) of Prayer and Freedom Ministries at Hosanna! Church, a church of seven thousand members in Minneapolis–St. Paul, Minnesota. She was the founder and president of Soterion, a communications company dedicated to the healthcare industry. Mary has a passion for helping people encounter God and His goodness in the midst of trials and be empowered and set free to live out their destiny. She emerged from a breast cancer diagnosis in 1999 eager to share how God restored and transformed her life. Her deepest desire is to give away what she has freely received.

Mary is the author of *Grace for Each Hour: Through the Breast Cancer Journey* (Bethany House, 2005), *Hope for Tough Times* (Revell, 2009), *Peace for Each Hour* (Comfort Publishing, 2013) and *Jehovah-Rapha: The God Who Heals* (Shiloh Run Press, 2016). Her books inspire those suffering from physical, emotional, relational, and spiritual brokenness by helping them draw close to the heart of God. She founded and leads the Pray for the Cure cancer healing and discipleship ministry at Hosanna! where she also serves as a leader in the Sozo inner healing ministry and healing prayer ministry. She and her husband, Howie, have two adult children and two grandchildren and have been married for forty years.